HISTORY MAP BOOKS

THE MODERN WORLD SINCE 1917

Philip Sauvain

Basil Blackwell

Teacher's Notes

The Modern World has been designed to give examination students a clear and concise outline structure of the essential elements of modern world history since 1917. Inevitably some topics have had to be omitted, so that the significant events of the twentieth century can stand out in sufficient detail, to emphasise their dramatic effect on the shaping of the modern world.

The maps, graphs, diagrams and charts, which together form the backbone of this book, have been planned as simply as possible to ensure that the relevant facts are presented in an easily assimilated form. In particular the maps have been envisaged as a type of shorthand, or mnemonic, of particular value for students working towards an external examination.

It is anticipated that this book will be used in various ways: by some as an introduction to the subject; by others as a study framework to be amplified with the use of other teaching materials. It may also be of service as a revision summary. Above all it is a *history map book* designed to support, consolidate and clarify work undertaken from the textbook.

© Philip Sauvain

First published 1983

Basil Blackwell Publisher
108 Cowley Road
Oxford
OX4 1JF

ISBN 0 631 91470 6

Typesetting and Design by KAG Design, Basingstoke
Printed in Hong Kong

ACKNOWLEDGEMENTS

The author and publisher wish to thank the following for permission to reproduce photographs:

Popperfoto 11 top left, top right and bottom, 17, 20 centre and bottom, 52, 53, 78 left.

Contents

The War to End All Wars

The map on this page shows the countries of Europe as they were in July 1914, just before the start of the First World War. On the map on the opposite page you can see how the boundaries had altered by 1920. Only six years had passed but Europe had radically changed. In 1914 all the big powers fighting in the war were ruled by a king or emperor, with the exception of France. By 1922 they were all republics except for Britain and Italy.

In 1914 there was widespread rejoicing in Berlin, London and Paris that, at last, a great war had begun.

Break-up of the Empires

Empires in 1914	Rulers in 1914	Empires in 1922	Republics in 1922
BRITISH	King George V	BRITISH	—
GERMAN	Kaiser William II	—	Republic (usually called the *Weimar Republic*) – Empire broken up
RUSSIAN	Tsar Nicholas II	—	Republic (later the *Union of Soviet Socialist Republics*) – Empire broken up
AUSTRO-HUNGARIAN	Emperor Francis Joseph	—	Republics of *Austria; Hungary; Czechoslovakia; Yugoslavia* (with Serbia and Montenegro) – other parts of Empire to Poland, Italy and Romania
OTTOMAN (TURKISH)	Sultan Mohammed V	—	*Republic of Turkey* – Empire broken up

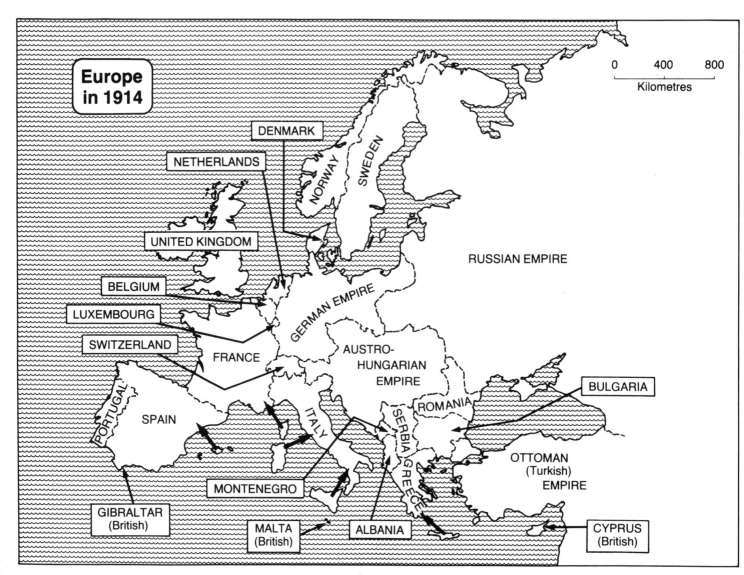

'A war to end all wars' people said. For years the main European powers had been preparing for such a war by building up their armies and weapons. When war came soldiers from the British and French empires also fought with the Allies against Germany, Austria, Hungary, Turkey and Bulgaria (the Central Powers) and were later joined by Japan, Italy, Romania, the United States, Brazil and other countries.

In March 1918 the Russians made a separate peace with the Germans at Brest-Litovsk. The other Allies fought on, aided now by the United States. The war finally ended at the eleventh hour, on the eleventh day, of the eleventh month in 1918.

Over eight million people had been killed and the countries of Europe had been ruined by the enormous expense and destruction of war. Workers went on strike and soldiers and sailors mutinied in several countries. The Bolshevik (Communist) Revolution in Russia in 1917 was followed by similar, but short-lived, revolutions in parts of Germany and in Hungary. The huge Austria-Hungary empire collapsed and several new nations were created in its place.

The New Countries of Europe after the First World War

New Country	In 1914 Part of:	Population	Capital City	Peoples
Finland	Russian Empire	3 million	Helsinki	Finns (90%)
Estonia	Russian Empire	1 million	Tallinn	Estonians (90%)
Latvia	Russian Empire	2 million	Riga	Letts (80%)
Lithuania	Russian Empire German Empire	2 million	Vilna (later Kaunas)	Lithuanians (90%)
Poland	Russian Empire German Empire Austro-Hungarian Empire	30 million	Warsaw	Poles (70%) Russians (15%) Germans (5%)
Czecho-slovakia	Austro-Hungarian Empire	13 million	Prague	Czechs and Slovaks (65%) Germans (25%)
Yugoslavia	Austro-Hungarian Empire Serbia Montenegro	12 million	Belgrade	Serbs and Croats (75%) Slovenes (10%)

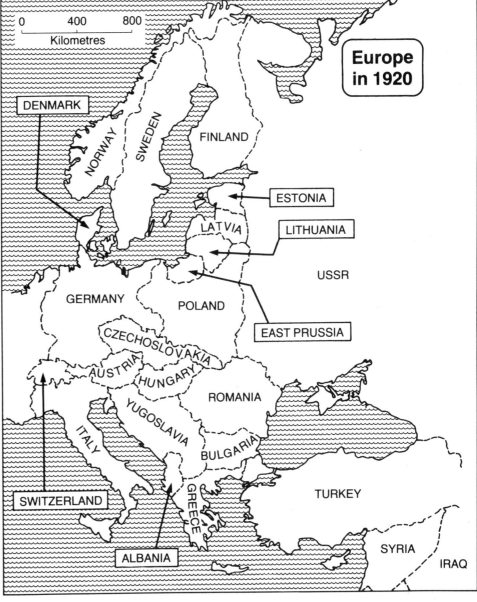

Europe in 1920

??????????????????
1 Why was it called a world war when most of the fighting took place in Europe and in the Middle East?
2 Compare the two maps. What were the main boundary changes in Europe after the war? Outline some of the other ways in which the First World War changed Europe.

The Russian Revolution

Diary of a Revolution

Up to 1917 the Russian people had had little say in the way they were governed. Most of the people lived a life of poverty. There was little freedom of speech and the *Okhrana* (secret police) ruthlessly hunted down opponents of the Tsar. An unsuccessful revolution in 1905 led to a few reforms, but many Russians felt that real change would only come about if the Tsar and his government were overthrown. Many of these revolutionaries had gone into exile in other countries or been sent to Siberia.

1916: Russia is in the middle of a disastrous war with Germany. Several million soldiers have been killed or wounded. The army is badly-led and badly-equipped. Foolishly, Tsar Nicholas II has taken command of the army, and is now blamed for its failures. Thousands of soldiers have mutinied or deserted. Food shortages at home have led to frequent strikes. The Royal Family is involved in scandal. The Tsarina relies heavily on a so-called holy man called Rasputin, whose evil influence is feared by many people.

7 March 1917: The Tsar takes no notice and leaves Petrograd (then the capital of Russia) to inspect his army.

8 March 1917: Bread shortages bring factory workers out on strike in Petrograd. The police and soldiers do little to stop the growing violence.

10 March 1917: About a quarter of a million workers are on strike. Troops mutiny and refuse to fire on the crowds.

30 December 1916: Rasputin is murdered by a group of patriotic nobles. They hope to restore the people's confidence in the Tsar.

January-February 1917: Railway breakdowns, price rises, shortages of food and fuel have made many people discontented. There are frequent strikes and demonstrations and the Tsar is warned there could be a revolution.

12 March 1917: Workers seize weapons, set fire to public buildings and sack police stations. The soldiers stationed at Petrograd cannot be relied on any longer. A provisional government is formed led by moderates. On the same day an alternative left-wing government is formed, called the Petrograd Soviet (Council) of Workers' and Soldiers' Deputies.

13 March 1917: Tsar Nicholas II tries to return to Petrograd but is stopped by demonstrators.

15 March 1917: The Tsar abdicates.

16 April 1917: Lenin, Trotsky and other left-wing leaders return to Russia from exile. Most are Bolsheviks – people who believe that the workers must seize power in a revolution. Lenin demands 'Peace, land and bread!' He wants to end the war, end poverty and let the peasants share out the land.

16 July 1917: The Bolsheviks try to overthrow the government, but the attempt fails. Many Bolsheviks (including Trotsky) are jailed and Lenin flees the country.

20 July 1917: Kerensky becomes Prime Minister. He appoints General Kornilov as commander of the army but Kornilov, fearful that Kerensky's government is too weak to stop the revolutionaries, tries to take over himself. Kerensky turns to the Bolsheviks for help. Kornilov's attempt to seize power is defeated by the newly-formed Bolshevik Red Guards.

October 1917: The Bolsheviks become more powerful whilst Kerensky's government becomes increasingly unpopular, since the war continues and food shortages are as bad as ever. There are many strikes. Lenin thinks the time is ripe for revolution.

7 November 1917: In the early hours of the morning Bolsheviks, Red Guards and mutinous soldiers seize key positions in Petrograd, such as the railway stations, telephone exchange, main bridges and post office. The warship 'Aurora' fires on the Winter Palace where the government is meeting. Kerensky has already fled but many of his ministers are arrested. Lenin leads the new government and the red flag flies over the Tsar's former palace.

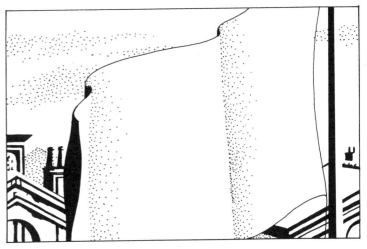

??????????????????????????

1 What were the causes of the first Russian Revolution in March 1917? Why did the second revolution follow only eight months later?

2 How did Lenin and the Bolsheviks overthrow the Provisional Government in the October Revolution? See if you can find out why the Russians called it the October Revolution when it took place in November.

The Paris Peace Conferences

Germany was forced to sign the Treaty of Versailles at the Paris Peace Conference in June 1919. The terms were dictated by the Allies. There was no discussion. As a result Germany had to surrender about 10 per cent of her territory to other countries. Many Germans now found themselves living in non-German countries like Poland.

The Treaty of Versailles also founded the League of Nations (see page 22). Separate treaties were signed in Paris (1919-20) with the other Central Powers – Austria, Hungary, Bulgaria and Turkey. These treaties created the new nation states of Czechoslovakia and Yugoslavia.

In addition Germany had to agree:

1 Not to have an army of more than 100,000 men.
2 Not to conscript soldiers (force them by law to join the army).
3 Not to arm her forces with aircraft, submarines, tanks, heavy guns or more than a certain number of warships.
4 Not to station troops in the Rhineland on the border with France, Belgium and the Netherlands.
5 Not to form a union (called Anschluss) with German-speaking Austria.
6 To lose her overseas colonies.
7 To pay a huge sum of money (equal to at least £70,000 million today) to help pay for the damage caused by the war. This was called Reparations and it had to be paid in instalments – even though Germany had been made very poor by her war effort.
8 To admit she was guilty of starting the war in the first place (which was not strictly true).

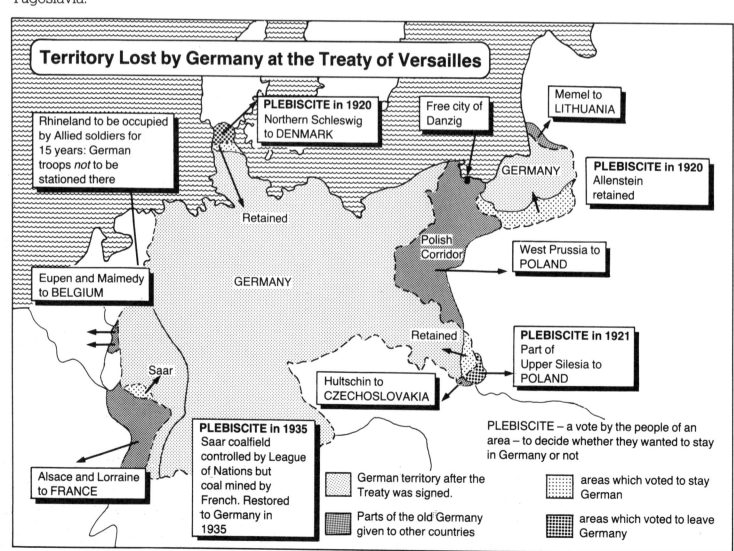

Territory Lost by Germany at the Treaty of Versailles

Rhineland to be occupied by Allied soldiers for 15 years: German troops *not* to be stationed there

PLEBISCITE in 1920 Northern Schleswig to DENMARK

Free city of Danzig

Memel to LITHUANIA

GERMANY

PLEBISCITE in 1920 Allenstein retained

Retained

Polish Corridor

West Prussia to POLAND

Eupen and Malmedy to BELGIUM

GERMANY

Saar

Retained

PLEBISCITE in 1921 Part of Upper Silesia to POLAND

Hultschin to CZECHOSLOVAKIA

Alsace and Lorraine to FRANCE

PLEBISCITE in 1935 Saar coalfield controlled by League of Nations but coal mined by French. Restored to Germany in 1935

PLEBISCITE – a vote by the people of an area – to decide whether they wanted to stay in Germany or not

German territory after the Treaty was signed.

areas which voted to stay German

Parts of the old Germany given to other countries

areas which voted to leave Germany

During the war several countries had been promised territory if they fought with the Allies. Not all were satisfied with the share-out.

ITALY had been promised Albania and also parts of the German empire in Africa. Mussolini later used this as an excuse to invade Albania and Abyssinia.

JAPAN was made to give up parts of China she had captured from the Germans in 1914. This was also used as an excuse when the Japanese invaded China in 1937.

Many of Germany's colonies were held by the countries who had captured them during the war. They continued to hold them as mandates from the League of Nations. Similar mandates from the old Turkish empire were given to France (Syria) and Britain (Iraq, Transjordan, Palestine).

How Austria-Hungary was Split up

former Austria-Hungary Empire

new nations created partly from territory which used to be part of the Austria-Hungary Empire

parts of the old Austria-Hungary Empire given to other countries

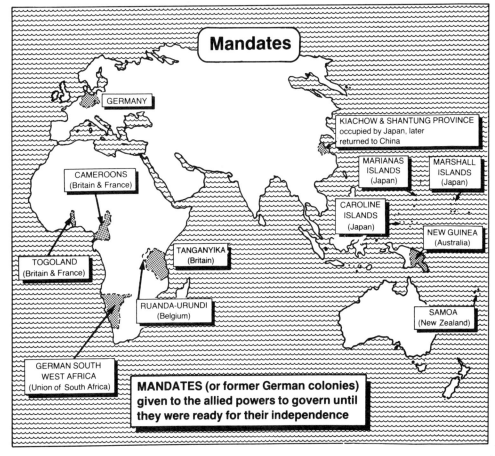

Mandates

KIACHOW & SHANTUNG PROVINCE occupied by Japan, later returned to China

MARIANAS ISLANDS (Japan)

MARSHALL ISLANDS (Japan)

CAROLINE ISLANDS (Japan)

NEW GUINEA (Australia)

CAMEROONS (Britain & France)

TANGANYIKA (Britain)

TOGOLAND (Britain & France)

RUANDA-URUNDI (Belgium)

SAMOA (New Zealand)

GERMAN SOUTH WEST AFRICA (Union of South Africa)

MANDATES (or former German colonies) given to the allied powers to govern until they were ready for their independence

??????????????????

1 Why do you think the Germans hated the Treaty of Versailles?

2 Which parts of the Treaty were designed to stop Germany starting another war?

3 Which of Germany's borders with other countries were the same after the Treaty as they were before the war?

Russia under Lenin

On 7 November 1917 Lenin formed the first communist government in Russia. Elections were held for a new assembly but Lenin closed it when the Social Revolutionary Party got twice as many seats as the Bolsheviks. Almost immediately Lenin began to carry out his promise of 'Peace, land and bread'. Land was to be taken from the landowners without compensation and shared out among the peasants. Important industries were to be controlled by the workers.

Landmarks of Lenin's Rule

The Cheka   In December 1917 Lenin set up a secret police called the Cheka. When an assassination attempt was made on his life the Cheka exterminated many of his opponents in the Red Terror.

Peace at any price   Roughly one soldier in every two had been killed or wounded in the war. The Russians wanted peace at any price. Trotsky went to Brest-Litovsk and in March 1918 signed a peace treaty with Germany. Russia was to lose Finland, Estonia, Latvia, Lithuania, most of the Ukraine and most of Poland. This was about a third of her total farmland, a third of her peoples and two-thirds of her coal and iron. However, the Treaty was quashed when Germany surrendered in November 1918.

Civil War   The Treaty annoyed many moderate Russians, as well as the Tsar's supporters and people who had lost their land or businesses. Lenin's opponents grew in number. The Allies were also annoyed by the Treaty since it meant that Germany was now free to concentrate on the war against them. They were also afraid communism might spread; so they sent troops to support the White Armies which were now gathering in opposition to the Bolsheviks. A bloody Civil War followed from 1917 to 1920. Hundreds of thousands of Russians died, many of them were killed or died from famine later on.

The Red Army   Trotsky as War Commissar built up the Red Army from a small fighting unit into an efficient army of several million soldiers. He toured the country in a huge train whipping up support for the Red Army. He emphasised the fact that many of Bolshevik Russia's enemies were foreign soldiers. By 1921 the Red Army was victorious and most of the foreign troops had been driven out of Russia.

War Communism   Lenin needed food for the Red Army; so he began a policy, called war communism, under which the peasants had to hand over all their surplus corn as a food tax. This was extremely unpopular and many peasants simply hid it, sold it privately against the law, or did not bother to grow any extra. Food shortages caused many deaths from starvation. Widespread unrest led to a serious mutiny of sailors at Kronstadt in 1921.

New Economic Policy   The riots made Lenin change his policy. He stopped the food tax. Peasants were now allowed to sell their surplus produce. Some private ownership of land and small businesses was also permitted. This was *not* communism, since it encouraged people to make a profit for their own benefit. But it did help the USSR to recover from the disastrous effects of the Civil War.

Communists believe:

★ That there has always been a *class struggle* between rich and poor; between capitalist (factory owner) and proletariat (industrial worker); between landowner and labourer.

★ That a workers' revolution is inevitable (sure to come). When it does the workers will take over the government. Karl Marx, the founder of modern communism, called this the *Dictatorship of the Proletariat*.

★ Eventually all the means of production (ways of making things – such as factories and farms) will be owned by the people in a *Socialist State*.

★ True *Communism* will come when there are no classes, and people do their best work but only receive payment according to their actual needs.

?????????????????????????

1   In what ways was Lenin a dictator? Did he rule with the consent of the people? What happened to his opponents?
2   How important was Trotsky to the success of the Bolshevik Revolution? What were his main achievements?

Leaders of the Russian Revolution

Stalin   1879-1953

Real name Joseph Vissarionovitch Dzhugashvili. A revolutionary from 1901 onwards. Disliked Trotsky. When Lenin died he cunningly schemed to become leader in 1927. Ruthlessly exterminated those who got in his way. Dictator from 1929 to his death in 1953.

Lenin   1870-1924

Real name Vladimir Ilyich Ulyanov. Bolshevik leader from 1903 onwards. Ruled communist Russia as a dictator from 1917 to his early death in 1924. Russia's greatest hero.

Trotsky   1879-1940

Real name Lev Davidovich Bronstein. Founded the first Soviet in Petrograd in 1905. Chief organiser of the 1917 Revolution in November. Successfully organised the Red Army during the Civil War. Lost power when Lenin died and went into exile. Murdered by one of Stalin's agents in 1940 in Mexico.

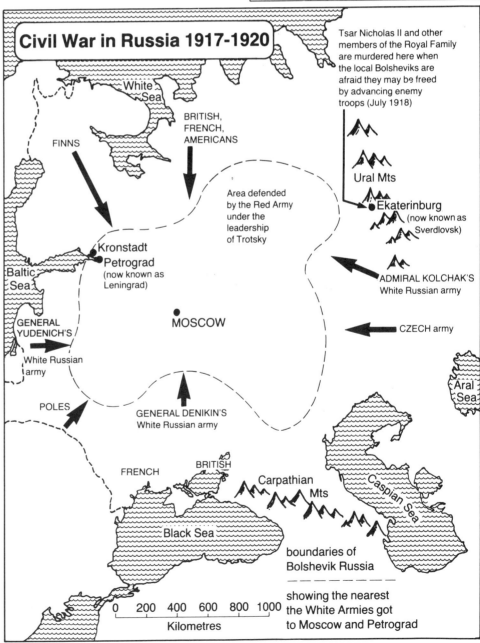

Civil War in Russia 1917-1920

White Sea

FINNS

BRITISH, FRENCH, AMERICANS

Tsar Nicholas II and other members of the Royal Family are murdered here when the local Bolsheviks are afraid they may be freed by advancing enemy troops (July 1918)

Ural Mts

Ekaterinburg (now known as Sverdlovsk)

Area defended by the Red Army under the leadership of Trotsky

ADMIRAL KOLCHAK'S White Russian army

Kronstadt
Petrograd (now known as Leningrad)

Baltic Sea

GENERAL YUDENICH'S
White Russian army

MOSCOW

CZECH army

POLES

GENERAL DENIKIN'S White Russian army

Aral Sea

FRENCH

BRITISH

Carpathian Mts

Caspian Sea

Black Sea

- - - boundaries of Bolshevik Russia

showing the nearest the White Armies got to Moscow and Petrograd

| 0 | 200 | 400 | 600 | 800 | 1000 |

Kilometres

The Roaring Twenties

When President Woodrow Wilson returned to the United States from the Paris Peace Conference, he tried unsuccessfully to get America to join the new League of Nations, which he had helped to found. But America was fed up with Europe. Over 100,000 American soldiers had died fighting to solve Europe's problems, not those of the United States. Many wanted to isolate America from these European quarrels. Warren Harding, a Republican, became President in 1920 with the slogan 'America First'.

This policy was called 'isolationism' and it lasted into the 1930s when Americans tried to ignore the threat to world peace posed by Nazi Germany. This is why the Americans did not enter the Second World War until December 1941.

The period from 1920 to 1929 is often called the 'Roaring Twenties' because it was a time of noise, lively action and growing prosperity. But although many people prospered in these 'boom years', the Republican slogans of 'a chicken in every pot' and 'a car in every garage' fell on deaf ears in many parts of America, as you can see from the map.

Boom Years in the United States

1920	Each symbol = 1 million	1930
🚗🚗🚗🚗 🚗🚗🚗🚗	CARS	🚗🚗🚗🚗🚗🚗🚗 🚗🚗🚗🚗🚗🚗🚗 🚗🚗🚗🚗🚗🚗🚗
📻 Very few	RADIOS	📻📻📻📻📻📻📻📻 📻📻

?????????????????????????
1 Give three reasons why the United States was prosperous in the 1920s.
2 What was meant by (a) isolationism (b) prohibition (c) the Wall Street Crash?

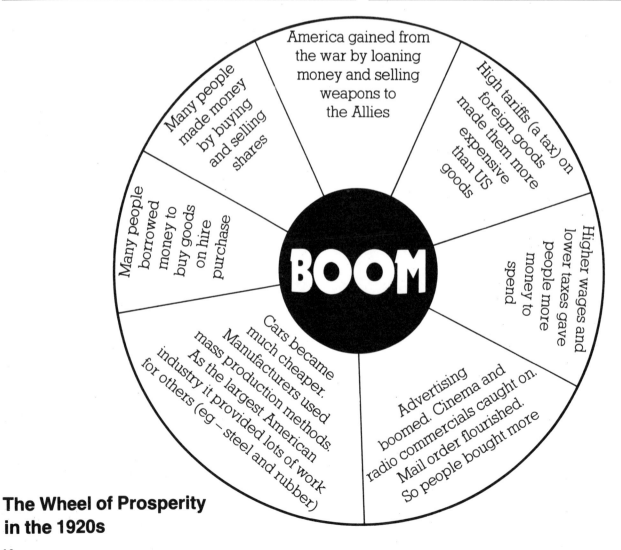

The Wheel of Prosperity in the 1920s

- America gained from the war by loaning money and selling weapons to the Allies
- High tariffs (a tax) on foreign goods made them more expensive than US goods
- Higher wages and lower taxes gave people more money to spend
- Advertising boomed. Cinema and radio commercials caught on. Mail order flourished. So people bought more
- Cars became much cheaper. Manufacturers used mass production methods. As the largest American industry it provided lots of work for others (eg – steel and rubber)
- Many people borrowed money to buy goods on hire purchase
- Many people made money by buying and selling shares

BOOM

The Great Wall Street Crash

Summer 1929 Shares on the New York Stock Exchange (in Wall Street) continue to go up in value, as they have been doing for several years now. Your friends have made money by buying shares and then selling them when the price has gone up. You borrow 1000 dollars from a bank and buy shares in a company.

29 October 1929 People have been selling a lot of shares recently because of signs of a downturn in the economy; suddenly everyone panics and 16 million shares are sold in a day. Because so many are for sale prices fall to rock bottom. You sell your shares for 200 dollars. Like thousands of others you have gone 'bust'.

November 1929 You tell the bank you cannot repay the 1000 dollars. Others, who have lost money on their shares, are also unable to repay their loans. People with savings in the bank try to withdraw their money but the bank has no cash left and has to shut.

1930-1932 There is little extra money about, so people stop buying luxury goods. Factories close. Millions become unemployed and cannot buy the essentials they need. Consequently many other factories also have to shut down. The boom is over; the depression has begun.

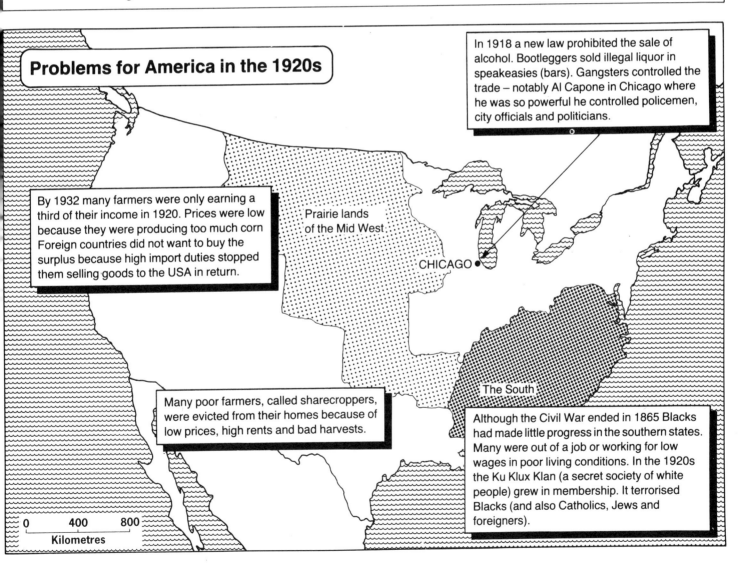

Problems for America in the 1920s

In 1918 a new law prohibited the sale of alcohol. Bootleggers sold illegal liquor in speakeasies (bars). Gangsters controlled the trade – notably Al Capone in Chicago where he was so powerful he controlled policemen, city officials and politicians.

By 1932 many farmers were only earning a third of their income in 1920. Prices were low because they were producing too much corn Foreign countries did not want to buy the surplus because high import duties stopped them selling goods to the USA in return.

Prairie lands of the Mid West

CHICAGO

Many poor farmers, called sharecroppers, were evicted from their homes because of low prices, high rents and bad harvests.

The South

Although the Civil War ended in 1865 Blacks had made little progress in the southern states. Many were out of a job or working for low wages in poor living conditions. In the 1920s the Ku Klux Klan (a secret society of white people) grew in membership. It terrorised Blacks (and also Catholics, Jews and foreigners).

0   400   800
Kilometres

Mussolini and Fascism

Benito Mussolini was the Fascist dictator of Italy from 1922 to 1943. The Italians called him 'Il Duce' (the Leader). In his youth he believed in socialism, pacifism (peace not war), atheism (that there is no God) and republicanism (having a president not a king). But when he became Italy's ruler he was anti-communist, a warmonger and a supporter of the Italian King and the Pope.

At first he brought prosperity to Italy and people were prepared to ignore the nastier side of Fascism.

But the Depression in the 1930s hit the Italians hard. Over a million workers were unemployed in 1932 compared with about 100,000 in 1925. By 1936 Mussolini's foreign adventures in Abyssinia and in the Spanish Civil War were leading Italy into trouble and eventually into world war, fighting alongside Hitler's Germany. In 1945 he fell into the hands of Italian partisans who were fighting the Germans. He was ignominiously executed.

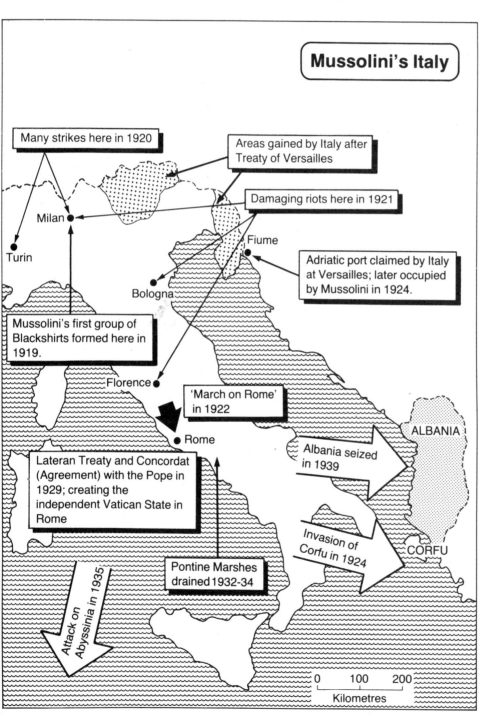

Mussolini's Italy

Many strikes here in 1920

Areas gained by Italy after Treaty of Versailles

Damaging riots here in 1921

Milan

Turin

Fiume

Adriatic port claimed by Italy at Versailles; later occupied by Mussolini in 1924.

Bologna

Mussolini's first group of Blackshirts formed here in 1919.

Florence

'March on Rome' in 1922

ALBANIA

Rome

Albania seized in 1939

Lateran Treaty and Concordat (Agreement) with the Pope in 1929; creating the independent Vatican State in Rome

Invasion of Corfu in 1924

CORFU

Pontine Marshes drained 1932-34

Attack on Abyssinia in 1935

0   100   200
Kilometres

Landmarks in Fascist Italy

1919: Mussolini formed the first of the *Fasci di Combattimento* ('Groups of Fighters'). They wore black uniforms and many were thugs and bully-boys. They adopted the *fasces* as their symbol. In Ancient Rome these were rods tied together in a bundle with an axe and used as a sign of authority.

1920-22: The Blackshirts broke up Communist meetings and workers strikes. There was a lot of street violence and hundreds of people were killed.

1922: A general strike led to a demand by Mussolini for the overthrow of the Government. His ill-equipped Blackshirts began the 'March on Rome' which could easily have been put down by the Army. Instead the King, fearing revolution, accepted the resignation of his Prime Minister and offered the job to Mussolini, long before the Blackshirts entered the capital.

1924: Giacomo Matteoti, a Socialist critic of the Fascist government, was brutally murdered in an attempt to quell opposition.

1925: Mussolini became a dictator, and only one political party, the Fascist, was permitted in Italy.

Conditions which helped Mussolini to Become Dictator

Cost of buying the same thing

Rising prices create unrest.

	94 lira
24 lira	

1915 1921

Many strikes.

Nationalists annoyed because Italy's demands for territory not met in full by Treaty of Versailles.

The Italian Government is weak and badly led.

Riots and street battles between Fascists and Communists.

Large numbers unemployed.

Groups of Communist workers form Soviets like those in Russia. Many fear a Bolshevik revolution in Italy.

Lots of dissatisfied ex-soldiers welcome opportunity to wear uniforms and attend Blackshirt rallies of Fascists.

Mussolini's Reforms

Land Reclamation	Reclaimed wasteland and boggy land and turned it into good farmland. In 1932-34 successfully drained the malarial Pontine Marshes.		
Transport	Electrified railways ('made the trains run on time') and built motorways (called *autostrada*).		
Education	Improved educational standards by making schools available to all. The number of children in secondary schools doubled in 17 years from 383,000 to 850,000.	**1922** 𝄞𝄞𝄞𝄞	**1939** 𝄞𝄞𝄞𝄞𝄞𝄞𝄞𝄞
		(each symbol = 100,000 pupils)	
Agriculture	Encouraged the use of new farming methods and declared there was a 'battle for wheat'.		
		(each symbol = 1 million tonnes of *wheat*)	
Industry	Gave State aid to industry; made the unions and management work together; banned strikes.		
		(each symbol = ¼ million tonnes of *steel*)	
Public Works	Built blocks of flats and offices, hydro-electric dams, bridges and other public buildings.		

Sayings of Mussolini and the Fascists

★ 'For Fascism the State is all-powerful' (Mussolini)
★ 'Believe! Obey! Fight!' (Fascist slogan)
★ 'Mussolini is always right' (Fascist slogan)
★ 'I want to make the people of Italy strong, prosperous, great and free' (Mussolini)
★ 'War is to the MAN what having children is to the WOMAN' (Fascist slogan)

?????????????????????????

1 What arguments do you think an Italian Fascist might have used to try to persuade you to support Mussolini (a) in 1922 before the March on Rome, (b) in 1939 before the outbreak of the Second World War?

2 In what ways did Mussolini's Fascist system of government differ from that of a modern democracy?

Germany after 1918

Germany's defeat in the First World War was the main reason why Adolf Hitler and the Nazi Party rose to power in the 1930s. The harsh terms of the Treaty of Versailles were bitterly resented throughout Germany. The huge reparations Germany had to pay the Allies for war damage led to colossal price rises. In 1923 the German mark became almost worthless. People who had put their life's savings in a bank in January found they were not enough to buy a postage stamp in November. The lucky ones were those who had borrowed money to buy a house or factory in 1922 and could pay back their loan in 1923.

Inflation in Germany (1914–1923)

[How the cost of something worth 100 marks before the war went up and up in price.]

On this scale if the 1922 column is 17 centimetres long, the 1923 column should be 170,000 *kilometres* long or *FOUR* times round the world.

A column ONE BILLION (1,000,000,000) times longer than the 1922 column 15,000 BILLION

14,000

Year	Value
1914	100
1915	125
1916	165
1917	250
1918	290
1919	400
1920	1,000
1921	1,300
1922	14,000
1923	15,000 BILLION

Time Line

1918 End of First World War. Kaiser abdicates. Communist uprisings in Berlin.

1919 Communist revolt put down with force. New government meets in Weimar. Germany now a Republic with a President.

Germany reluctantly signs the Treaty of Versailles, by which she loses several territories and has to pay a large sum of money in compensation – reparations.

1923 Germany falls behind with her payments, so French troops seize the rich Ruhr coalfield. The miners strike, production is halted, the value of the German mark drops, huge price rises (inflation).

In *November* Adolf Hitler takes advantage of widespread misery and discontent and tries to seize power in Munich. His attempt fails and 16 of his Nazi storm troopers (the SA) are killed and he is gaoled. Goering is seriously wounded.

1924 Hitler writes *Mein Kampf* in prison, with the assistance of Rudolf Hess. It later becomes the bible of the Nazi Party.

Meanwhile Germany's money problems are so bad, a committee led by Charles Dawes, an American, recommends a large loan to Germany to stop the country going bankrupt.

1924 to 1929 Germany begins to prosper once more.

1926 She accepts the conditions laid down by the League of Nations for membership and becomes a permanent member of the Council.

??????????????????????????

1 What were the effects of inflation in Germany in 1923? By how many times did prices rise (a) between 1914 and 1918, (b) between 1918 and 1922, (c) between 1922 and 1923?

2 What were the conditions which encouraged Hitler and the Nazi Party to think the time was ripe to seize power in Munich in 1923?

Adolf Hitler 1889-1945

Born in Austria. Lived in poverty in the slums of Vienna. Emigrated to Germany (Munich) in 1913. Fought bravely in the war, winning the Iron Cross. In 1919 joined the German Workers' Party (it had only 40 members). Hitler soon got attention as a brilliant speaker. Their policies were announced on 1 April 1920 as the *Twenty-Five Points*. They included a demand for an end to the terms of the Versailles Treaty, union of all German people in one German nation (Hitler was an Austrian citizen until 1932), and foreign territory to give Germany the space needed for a growing population. They were also anti-Semitic (against the Jews) and stressed the duties of the citizen to the State and not the rights of the individual. Soon afterwards it was renamed the Nationalist Socialist German Workers' Party (NSDAP), or Nazi Party as it came to be known.

The Twenty Five Points were the starting-point for Hitler's book *Mein Kampf* (My Struggle), which he wrote when imprisoned after the failure of the Munich 'Putsch'. From 1924-29 Hitler and his followers (Goering, Himmler and Goebbels) reorganized the Nazi Party and prepared for their future victory.

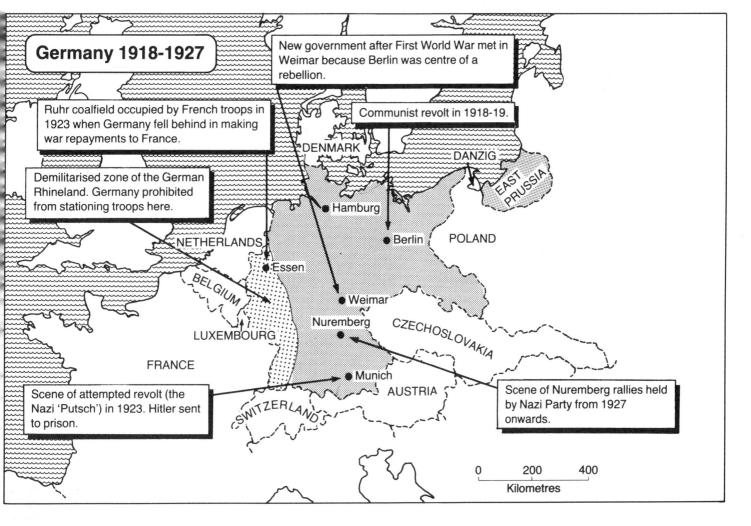

Germany 1918-1927

New government after First World War met in Weimar because Berlin was centre of a rebellion.

Ruhr coalfield occupied by French troops in 1923 when Germany fell behind in making war repayments to France.

Communist revolt in 1918-19.

Demilitarised zone of the German Rhineland. Germany prohibited from stationing troops here.

Scene of attempted revolt (the Nazi 'Putsch') in 1923. Hitler sent to prison.

Scene of Nuremberg rallies held by Nazi Party from 1927 onwards.

DENMARK · DANZIG · EAST PRUSSIA · Hamburg · Berlin · POLAND · NETHERLANDS · Essen · BELGIUM · Weimar · Nuremberg · CZECHOSLOVAKIA · LUXEMBOURG · FRANCE · Munich · AUSTRIA · SWITZERLAND

0   200   400
Kilometres

Stalin's Russia

In 1927 Joseph Stalin became leader of the USSR. **Stalin** means 'man of steel' and he proved it by ruthlessly stamping out any opposition. In 1928 he launched the first of his Five Year Plans which he hoped would make Russia a powerful industrial nation. Many large iron and steel works, hydro-electric dams and factories were built. Land was forcibly taken from the peasants and combined into large State farms or collective farms run by committees of workers. Well-to-do peasants (kulaks) who resisted these changes were either shot or sent to work in labour camps. Many peasants killed off their livestock rather than give them to the new collectives.

Stalin also faced opposition within the Communist Party, and in 1936-38 he began the Purges which eliminated his opponents and made him the undisputed leader of the Soviet Union.

Stalin's Aims

1 To produce more coal, oil and electricity to power the new heavy industries.
2 To build new iron and steel works and chemical plants to provide the raw materials needed to manufacture tanks, weapons, ammunition, machinery and essential goods.
3 To get more people to live in the towns to provide labour for the new factories.
4 To produce more food to feed Russia's growing population and the peasants who left the land to work in the factories.
5 To educate the people. In 1914 only four people in every ten could read or write; by 1939 it was nine out of ten.

Growth in Production during the First Twelve Years of Stalin's Five Year Plans		RATE OF INCREASE
COAL	36 million tonnes 1928 / 166 million tonnes 1940	4½ times as much
STEEL	4 million tonnes 1928 / 18 million tonnes 1940	4½ times as much
ELECTRICITY	5 billion kilowatt hours 1928 / 48 million kilowatt hours 1940	nearly 10 times as much
MOTOR VEHICLES	Very few vehicles 1928 / 145,000 vehicles 1940	about 150 times as much
LENGTH OF ROADS	32,000 km of surfaced road 1928 / 143,000 km of surfaced road 1940	4½ times as much

Why Stalin and Trotsky Disagreed

Trotsky
Wanted Russia to encourage communists in other countries to overthrow their governments.

Stalin
Preferred to make Russia strong and powerful at home first of all. Called it 'Socialism in one country'.

Sayings of Stalin

★ 'Put the peasant on a tractor and you have Socialism' (i.e: mechanisation is essential if communism is to succeed).
★ 'We must smash the kulaks'.
★ 'We are fifty years behind the advanced countries. We must catch up in ten years or they will attack us'.

Time Line

1924 Death of Lenin. Stalin, Kamenev and Zinoviev (not Trotsky) become the most important leaders in the Party.

1927 Trotsky and Zinoviev are expelled from the Party. Stalin becomes leader.

1928 Start of first Five Year Plan. Collectives are formed.

1929 Stalin rules as a dictator. Trotsky exiled from Russia.

1931 The countryside is in turmoil after the collectivisation of farming. The harvest fails and famine follows.

1933 Start of the second Five Year Plan.

1936 The Purges begin. The NKVD (secret police) extract confessions. Show trials are held and many powerful Communist Party officials are executed, including Kamenev and Zinoviev. Eight million people are arrested and one million are executed, including twenty-three leading Soviet generals – depriving the Red Army of some of its best leaders.

1938 The Purges end. All opposition to Stalin is crushed.

The Effect of the Collectives on Russian Farming

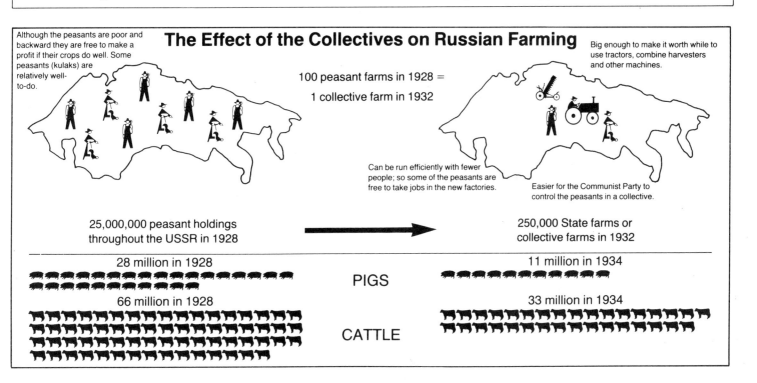

Although the peasants are poor and backward they are free to make a profit if their crops do well. Some peasants (kulaks) are relatively well-to-do.

100 peasant farms in 1928 = 1 collective farm in 1932

Big enough to make it worth while to use tractors, combine harvesters and other machines.

Can be run efficiently with fewer people; so some of the peasants are free to take jobs in the new factories.

Easier for the Communist Party to control the peasants in a collective.

25,000,000 peasant holdings throughout the USSR in 1928 → 250,000 State farms or collective farms in 1932

PIGS	
28 million in 1928	11 million in 1934

CATTLE	
66 million in 1928	33 million in 1934

???????????????????????????

1 How and why did Stalin introduce collective farms? What happened when the kulaks resisted these changes?

2 How and at what cost did Stalin improve Russian industry? What did he hope to achieve?

3 How did Stalin deal with his political opponents in Russia? What happened to Trotsky and other leaders of the Party who were important when Lenin was alive? What was Stalin afraid of?

Roosevelt and the New Deal

The great depression of the 1930s was not entirely due to the Wall Street Crash in October 1929. American factories had been producing too many goods and found it difficult to sell abroad. The high tariffs (import duties) on foreign goods did not encourage other countries to buy American exports in return. Although the United States had followed a policy of isolationism, she had continued to lend money to the countries of Europe to stop them going bankrupt. Now the effects of the Depression were so bad the Americans tried to recover some of the money they had lent to other countries. This had the effect of causing a severe slump (or depression) in trade across the world. You can see the effect it had on Germany on page 24.

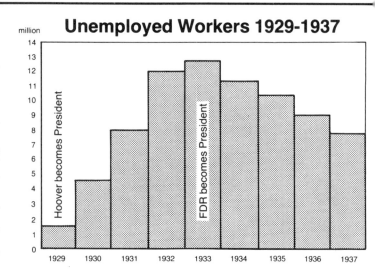

Unemployed Workers 1929-1937

million

(bar chart showing unemployed workers in millions from 1929 to 1937: 1929 ≈ 1.5, 1930 ≈ 4.5, 1931 ≈ 8, 1932 ≈ 12, 1933 ≈ 12.5, 1934 ≈ 11, 1935 ≈ 10.5, 1936 ≈ 9, 1937 ≈ 7.5. "Hoover becomes President" marked at 1929, "FDR becomes President" marked at 1933.)

Herbert Hoover   President of the USA   1929-1933

Self-made millionaire who believed in self-help. During the trade depression, he refused to give direct government aid to the unemployed. Since there was no unemployment benefit the cities were filled with destitute people 'standing in line' for a free meal. Hoover told the people that 'prosperity is around the corner' but he did little to help it on its way.

Franklin Delano Roosevelt   President of the USA   1933-1945

FDR, as popularly known, came from a rich family. He was crippled with polio when 39. Promised the voters at the 1932 Presidential Election that he would give them 'a new deal'. His first hundred days in office in 1933 were remarkable for a large number of important new reforms which cut unemployment and gave Americans a sense of purpose. Also introduced sick pay, unemployment and old age benefits. He was unpopular with the wealthy who had to pay higher taxes to pay for his projects, and with those who, like Hoover, believed people should stand on their own feet. Annoyed big firms with his trade union reforms. Some critics called him a communist and others a fascist! The voters elected him President for a record FOUR terms in office. He died in 1945, when he was still President, but before the end of the Second World War.

The Alphabet Agencies of the New Deal

AAA AGRICULTURAL ADJUSTMENT ACT 1933
Allowed the government to control farm prices and to pay farmers to stop producing so much food.

CCC CIVILIAN CONSERVATION CORPS 1933
Employed jobless youths from the slums in conservation camps – building roads, clearing land and planting trees.

CWA CIVIL WORKS ADMINISTRATION 1933
Gave work to about four million unemployed on various government projects.

NRA NATIONAL RECOVERY ADMINISTRATION 1933
Tried to improve working conditions in factories.

REA RURAL ELECTRIFICATION ADMINISTRATION 1935
Set up to bring electricity to country areas.

TVA TENNESSEE VALLEY AUTHORITY 1933
Imaginative scheme to control flooding on the Tennessee River by building a series of dams, which could also be used to produce hydro-electricity.

WPA WORKS PROGRESS ADMINISTRATION 1935
Completed thousands of new projects, such as dams, tunnels, bridges and hospitals. Employed millions of workers on projects of great value to all Americans.

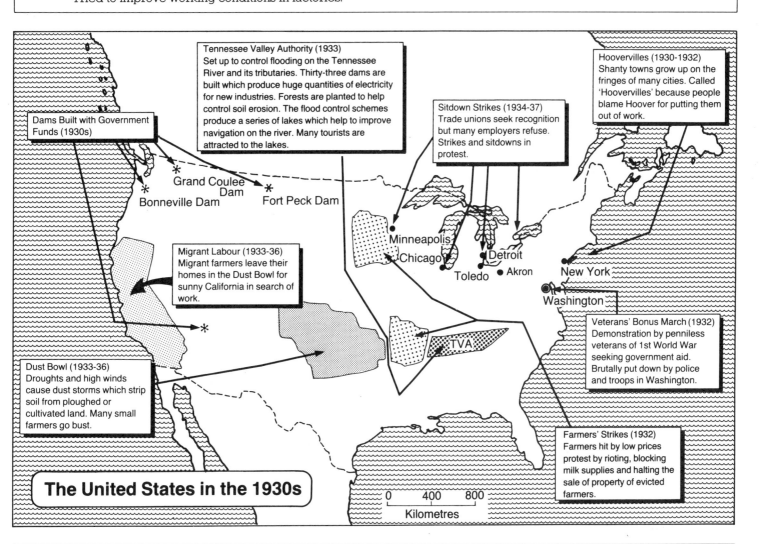

The United States in the 1930s

Tennessee Valley Authority (1933)
Set up to control flooding on the Tennessee River and its tributaries. Thirty-three dams are built which produce huge quantities of electricity for new industries. Forests are planted to help control soil erosion. The flood control schemes produce a series of lakes which help to improve navigation on the river. Many tourists are attracted to the lakes.

Dams Built with Government Funds (1930s)

Grand Coulee Dam
Bonneville Dam
Fort Peck Dam

Migrant Labour (1933-36)
Migrant farmers leave their homes in the Dust Bowl for sunny California in search of work.

Dust Bowl (1933-36)
Droughts and high winds cause dust storms which strip soil from ploughed or cultivated land. Many small farmers go bust.

Sitdown Strikes (1934-37)
Trade unions seek recognition but many employers refuse. Strikes and sitdowns in protest.

Hoovervilles (1930-1932)
Shanty towns grow up on the fringes of many cities. Called 'Hoovervilles' because people blame Hoover for putting them out of work.

Minneapolis
Chicago
Detroit
Toledo
Akron
New York
Washington

TVA

Veterans' Bonus March (1932)
Demonstration by penniless veterans of 1st World War seeking government aid. Brutally put down by police and troops in Washington.

Farmers' Strikes (1932)
Farmers hit by low prices protest by rioting, blocking milk supplies and halting the sale of property of evicted farmers.

0   400   800
Kilometres

???

1 Explain what was behind the words of this popular song of the 1930s:

'Why should I be standing in line, just waiting for bread?
Once I built a railroad; now it's done.
Brother can you spare a dime?'

2 Why did Roosevelt say in a speech in the 1930s: 'It is true that the toes of some people are being stepped on and are going to be stepped on'? What was the 'new deal' he promised the American people?

The League of Nations

President Wilson of the United States suggested the founding of a League of Nations in January 1918 as a way of trying to keep the peace when the First World War was over. A Covenant (promise) to start the League of Nations was made part of the Paris Peace Treaties in 1919. Ironically the United States was one of the few countries *not* to join the League of Nations when it began work in Geneva in 1920.

Unfortunately the member countries often disagreed with each other. There was no way of making countries obey the League's decisions. Countries usually agreed to the League's decisions *provided* they did not affect themselves. With minor disputes the League had several successes. But when the permanent members of the Council became the aggressors, Japan (1931) and Italy (1935), the League could not stop them. It also suffered because the world's most powerful nation, the United States, never became a member. On many issues the League failed because its decisions usually had to be unanimous, and members would not agree.

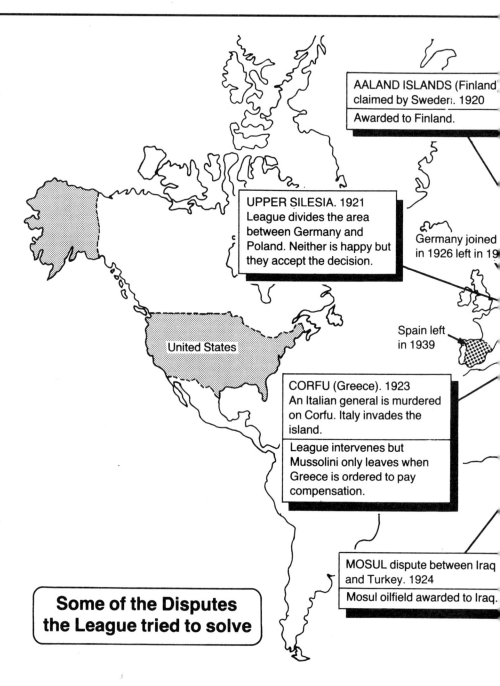

AALAND ISLANDS (Finland) claimed by Sweden. 1920

Awarded to Finland.

UPPER SILESIA. 1921
League divides the area between Germany and Poland. Neither is happy but they accept the decision.

Germany joined in 1926 left in 19

Spain left in 1939

CORFU (Greece). 1923
An Italian general is murdered on Corfu. Italy invades the island.

League intervenes but Mussolini only leaves when Greece is ordered to pay compensation.

MOSUL dispute between Iraq and Turkey. 1924

Mosul oilfield awarded to Iraq.

United States

Some of the Disputes the League tried to solve

Aims of the League of Nations

The member nations agreed:

1 To do their best to stop war.
2 To keep existing boundaries between nations.
3 To ensure that all member-countries kept their independence.
4 To try to get disarmament (the reduction in the number of weapons in a country) agreed.
5 To co-operate on matters which concerned everyone, such as health and the care of refugees.

6 To use sanctions if any country attacked another without good cause. Sanctions were a way of trying to force a country to accept the League's decisions. Sanctions could mean all member-countries refusing to trade with a country *or* even the use of armed force. This was called *collective security* because the member countries decided to act collectively (i.e., together).

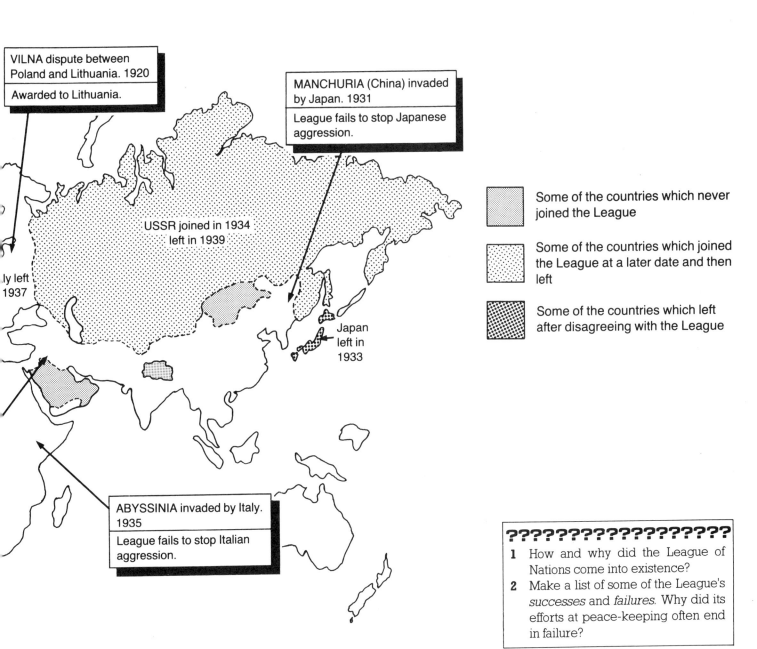

VILNA dispute between Poland and Lithuania. 1920
Awarded to Lithuania.

MANCHURIA (China) invaded by Japan. 1931
League fails to stop Japanese aggression.

USSR joined in 1934
left in 1939

...ly left
1937

Japan
left in
1933

ABYSSINIA invaded by Italy. 1935
League fails to stop Italian aggression.

Some of the countries which never joined the League

Some of the countries which joined the League at a later date and then left

Some of the countries which left after disagreeing with the League

???????????????????

1 How and why did the League of Nations come into existence?

2 Make a list of some of the League's *successes* and *failures*. Why did its efforts at peace-keeping often end in failure?

Organisation of the League of Nations

Secretariat
Officials who ran the League from its headquarters in Geneva.

Council
Met several times a year. Originally consisted of four permanent members: Britain, France, Italy (left in 1937), Japan (left in 1933). Germany became the fifth member in 1926 but left in 1933. Her place was taken by the USSR in 1934 but she was expelled by the other countries in 1939. There were also four (and later nine) members elected by the General Assembly.

General Assembly
Met once a year. Each country had the right to send a delegate and had one vote whatever its size.

Court of International Justice
Met at the Hague in the Netherlands. The 15 judges from different countries had to decide any disputes which were brought before them.

International Labour Organisation (ILO)
Tried to improve working conditions in factories throughout the world.

Other Organisations were concerned with world health, minorities, mandated territories, disarmament, refugees, slavery, loans to poorer countries.

The Rise of Hitler

The diagram below shows why millions of Germans voted Hitler into power in 1933. Nearly six million Germans (about one worker in every three) was out of a job by then. Communism and Fascism both seemed to promise a solution. In the November 1932 elections the Communists gained 100 seats in the Reichstag to the Nazis' 196 seats.

Unemployment in Germany (1929-1939)

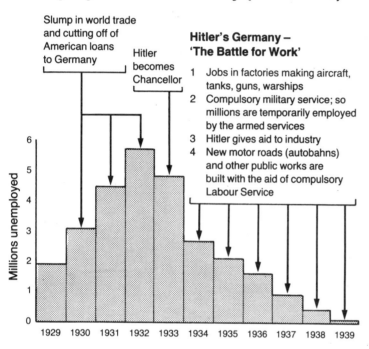

How Hitler became the Führer

1 The violence on the streets between Hitler's storm troopers – SS (Blackshirts) and SA (Brownshirts) – and Communists and other opponents led many people to welcome a party with military discipline.

2 Hitler's election meetings were attended by huge crowds; he was a brilliant speaker. An American saw a crowd with 'crazed expressions' looking up to him 'as if he were a Messiah'.

3 Hitler promised jobs when he spoke to the workers *but* an end to strikes to industrialists (when they paid for his election campaigns).

4 Soon after the Nazi Party became the largest group in the Reichstag, Hitler was invited to become Chancellor (the German Prime Minister).

5 Within two months an Enabling Law (which was permitted under the German Constitution) was passed allowing him to rule Germany as a dictator (March 1933).

6 When President Hindenburg died, he became the 'Führer' (Leader), just as Mussolini had become 'Il Duce' (Leader).

Propaganda

Hitler's propaganda minister, *Josef Goebbels*, used newspapers, films and broadcasts to drum up popular support. There were annual Nuremberg rallies, goose-stepping parades, torchlight processions, stirring music, flags and banners, shouts of 'Sieg Heil!' and the slogan 'Ein Volk, ein Reich, ein Führer!' (One People, one Country, one Leader!). They excited the German people and made them proud to be Germans. 'The great mass of the people are more likely to believe a big lie than a little one' said Hitler. 'All Germany listens to the Führer' was the advertising slogan for a radio!

Fascists believe in:

1 **Totalitarianism:** *one* leader to inspire the people; *one* political party; everyone has a *duty* to serve the State; the rights of individuals are not important.

2 **Nationalism** and pride in one's country.

3 **Anti-Communism**

4 **Compulsory Military Service** and **Ritual Ceremonies** such as parades, marches, rallies, wearing of splendid uniforms.

5 **Positive Action:**
(a) taking aggressive steps to defend the State and to expand its frontiers, if this is in the interests of the people.
(b) using propaganda (press, advertisements, broadcasts) to convince people that Fascism is good for them. Educating children to believe in a good life under Fascism.
(c) using ruthless and sometimes violent methods to quell opposition – establishing a secret police, extracting confessions, using terror to make people afraid of voicing their opposition.
(d) using public works, such as building new roads, bridges and public buildings as a means of ending unemployment.

Hitler's Policy towards:

Jews   Persecuted. Property seized. Nuremberg Laws (1935) banned Jews from being German citizens, marrying Germans or voting in elections. During the Second World War six million Jews from all over Europe were taken to concentration camps, like Dachau, Belsen, Buchenwald and Auschwitz, for the 'Final Solution' – to be put to death.

Communists   Five communists were accused of starting the fire which destroyed the Reichstag (home of the German Parliament) soon after Hitler became Chancellor in 1933. This gave Hitler an excuse to ban the Communist Party and arrest thousands of its members and send them to concentration camps.

Trade Unions   Abolished. Leaders arrested and sent to concentration camps.

Other Political Parties   Persecuted and later banned. Germany became a One-Party State.

Churches   Persecuted. Many priests and nuns sent to concentration camps.

Education   Children taught to be good Nazis at an early age. Textbooks rewritten. Offending books burned. Hitler Youth founded – compulsory membership for all boys between 14 and 21. Similar organisations for girls and children between 8 and 14.

Fellow Nazis   Ruthlessly eliminated if thought to be a threat – executed Ernst Rohm and other SA leaders ('the Night of the Long Knives' – 30 June 1934).

Fellow Germans   Employed the Gestapo (secret police) to search out all opponents of his regime, using informers and torture to extract information.

The Nazis at the Polls

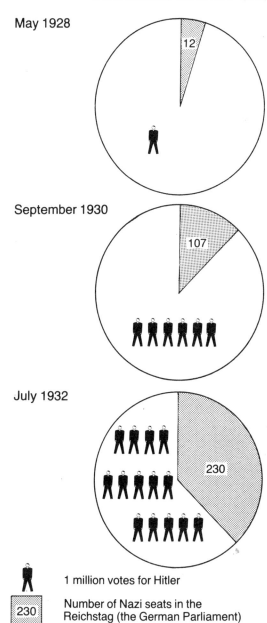

May 1928

September 1930

July 1932

 1 million votes for Hitler

230 Number of Nazi seats in the Reichstag (the German Parliament)

Heavy Industry Grows under Hitler

1933		1939 (Six years later)
● ● ● ● ● ● ● ● ● ● ● ● ● ● ● ● ● ● ● ● ● ● ● ● ● ● ●	**COAL** ● = 10 million tonnes	● ● ● ● ● ● ● ● ● ● ● ● ● ● ● ● ● ● ● ● ● ● ● ● ● ● ● ● ● ● ● ● ● ● ● ● ● ● ● ● ● ● ● ● ● ●
△ △ △ △ △ △ △ △	**STEEL** △ = 1 million tonnes	△ △ △ △ △ △ △ △ △ △ △ △ △ △ △ △ △ △ △ △ △ △ △ △ △
☐ ☐	**ALUMINIUM** ☐ = 10,000 tonnes	☐ ☐ ☐ ☐ ☐ ☐ ☐ ☐ ☐ ☐ ☐ ☐ ☐ ☐ ☐ ☐ ☐ ☐ ☐

??????????????????

1   How and why was Hitler able to become Chancellor of Germany in 1933?

2   How did he make sure that all opposition to the Nazi government was crushed?

3   In what ways was Hitler's Nazi Germany similar to Mussolini's Fascist Italy? How were they different?

The Chinese Revolution before 1937

In 1911 Chinese Nationalists, led by Sun Yat-sen, deposed the Emperor and turned China into a republic. But the new government in Peking could not control huge areas of China; these were at the mercy of the Warlords (generals with private armies). In 1917 the Nationalists (or *Kuomintang*) formed their own revolutionary government in Canton in southern China. In 1924 they agreed that Sun Yat-sen's 'Three Principles' should be the policy of the Party. They also agreed to admit communists into their party.

Sun Yat-sen's Three Principles

1 People should be able to vote for their leaders – DEMOCRACY.
2 The land should be fairly shared out among the people – SOCIALISM.
3 All foreign influence should go and China should become one nation – NATIONALISM.

When Sun Yat-sen died in 1925 his place was taken by the right-wing army general, Chiang Kai-shek.

Chiang Kai-shek 1887-1975

After the Northern March against the Warlords (see map), Chiang Kai-shek began to modernise central China in the area he controlled near the mouth of the Yantze Kiang, building railways, roads and modern factories. But he did not share out the land as Sun Yat-sen had promised the peasants. He ruled as a dictator. He did not manage to make China into one nation; instead he began a feud between Nationalists and Communists which lasted for over twenty years. For much of that time there was a bitter Civil War.

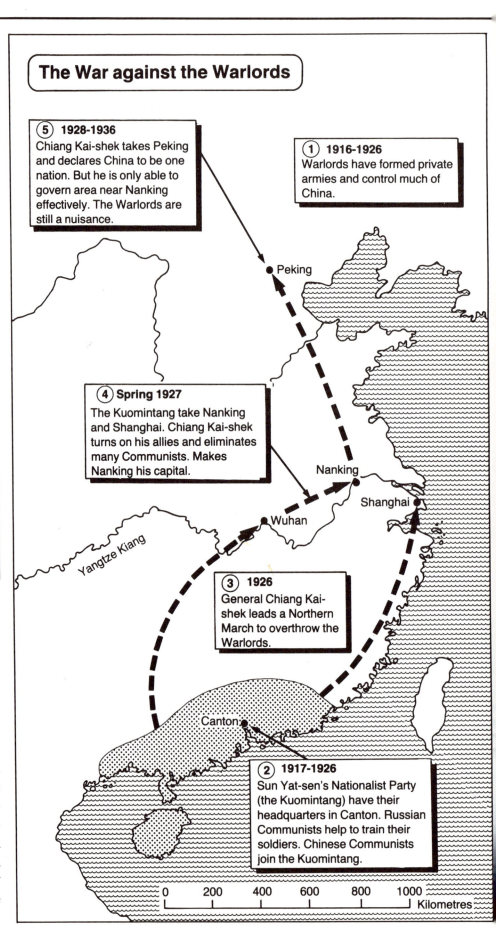

The War against the Warlords

⑤ **1928-1936**
Chiang Kai-shek takes Peking and declares China to be one nation. But he is only able to govern area near Nanking effectively. The Warlords are still a nuisance.

① **1916-1926**
Warlords have formed private armies and control much of China.

④ **Spring 1927**
The Kuomintang take Nanking and Shanghai. Chiang Kai-shek turns on his allies and eliminates many Communists. Makes Nanking his capital.

③ **1926**
General Chiang Kai-shek leads a Northern March to overthrow the Warlords.

② **1917-1926**
Sun Yat-sen's Nationalist Party (the Kuomintang) have their headquarters in Canton. Russian Communists help to train their soldiers. Chinese Communists join the Kuomintang.

Peking • Nanking • Shanghai • Wuhan • Canton • Yangtze Kiang

0 200 400 600 800 1000
Kilometres

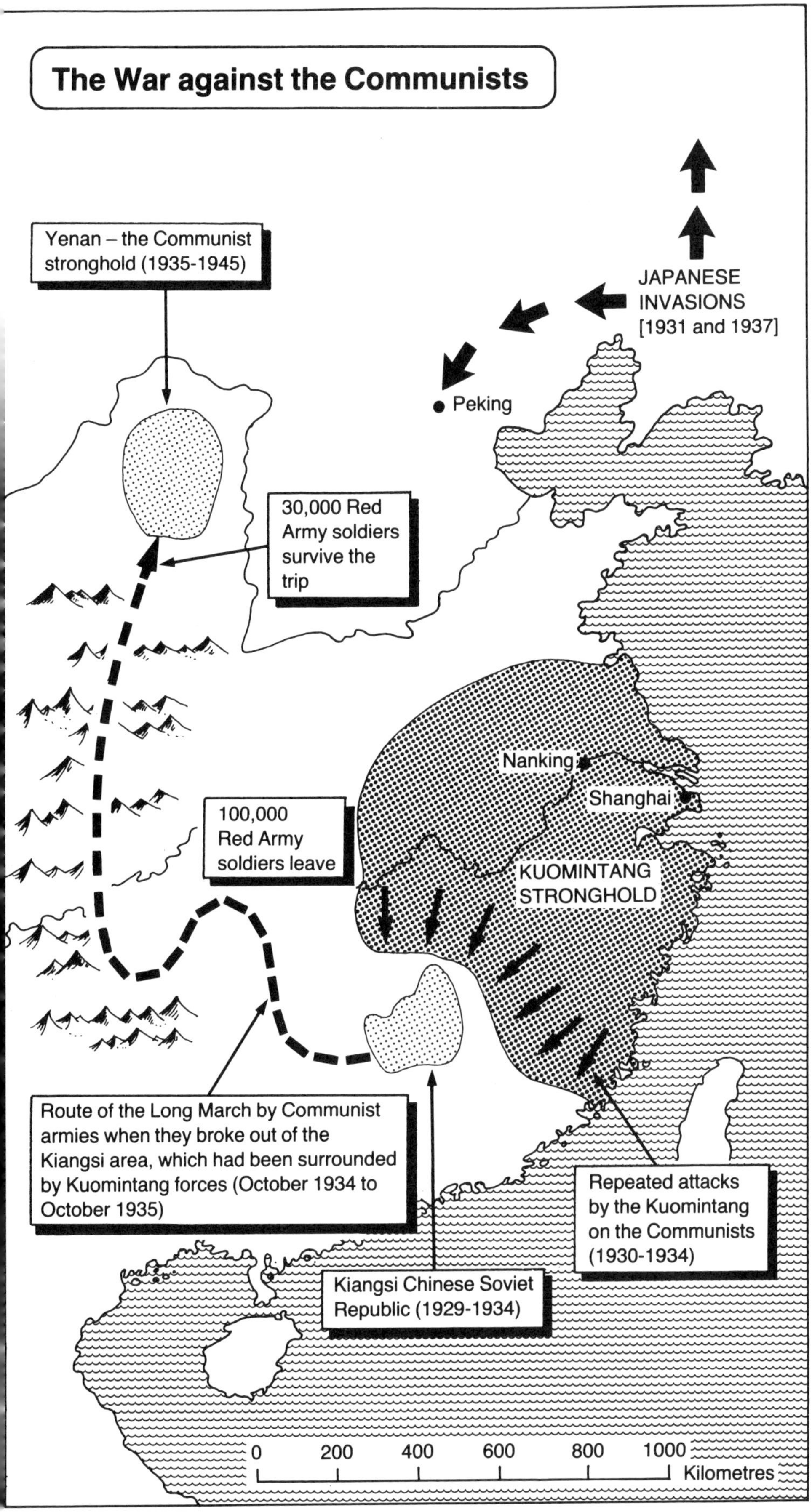

The War against the Communists

Yenan – the Communist stronghold (1935-1945)

JAPANESE INVASIONS [1931 and 1937]

• Peking

30,000 Red Army soldiers survive the trip

100,000 Red Army soldiers leave

Nanking

Shanghai

KUOMINTANG STRONGHOLD

Route of the Long March by Communist armies when they broke out of the Kiangsi area, which had been surrounded by Kuomintang forces (October 1934 to October 1935)

Repeated attacks by the Kuomintang on the Communists (1930-1934)

Kiangsi Chinese Soviet Republic (1929-1934)

0   200   400   600   800   1000
Kilometres

The Long March

The Chinese Communists, led by men like Mao Tse-tung and Chou En-lai, established a Chinese Soviet Republic in the mountains of southern China in 1929. Even though China was invaded by the Japanese in 1931, Chiang Kai-shek paid more attention to the Communists than to the foreign invaders. His Kuomintang forces tried again and again to drive the Communists out of their stronghold, but without success. Then they decided to surround the Communists with soldiers and starve them out. In October 1934 Mao and his colleagues decided it was time to break out of the Kiangsi area and make their way through the mountains of western China to another Communist stronghold in the north.

For 368 days Mao and the Red Army soldiers marched at a gruelling pace. Some days they travelled as much as 60 or even 100 kilometres in 24 hours. Eventually they reached their new home, only to face a new threat when Japan invaded China in 1937.

?????????????????????

1 What were Chiang Kai-shek's most important problems when he became leader of the Kuomintang? How did he try to solve these problems? (To answer this question fully, you will also have to study the section on Japan on pages 28-9.)

2 Why do you think the Chinese Communists and the Kuomintang both regarded the Long March as a victory for their own side?

War between China and Japan: 1931 and

Japan invaded Manchuria in 1931. She already had strong ties with the region and wanted Manchuria's rich reserves of oil, coal, iron ore, bauxite, magnesite, timber and other much-needed raw materials.

China appealed to the League of Nations for help. When the League eventually condemned Japan's action it was too late. The Japanese simply stopped being members of the League. So Japan got away without being punished, which was noticed by Mussolini, Hitler, and the Japanese generals who planned the invasion in the first place. Small countries could well worry about the future, since it was obvious the League of Nations was unable to guarantee international frontiers.

Chiang Kai-shek did little to oppose the Japanese but when they invaded China again in 1937, he and Mao Tse-tung jointly agreed to fight the invading Japanese.

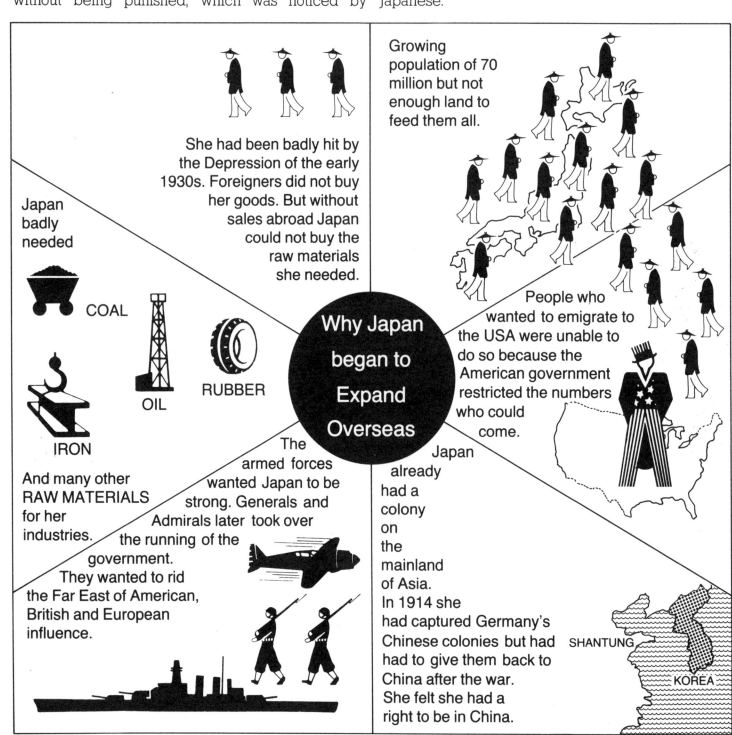

Growing population of 70 million but not enough land to feed them all.

She had been badly hit by the Depression of the early 1930s. Foreigners did not buy her goods. But without sales abroad Japan could not buy the raw materials she needed.

Japan badly needed

COAL

OIL

RUBBER

IRON

And many other RAW MATERIALS for her industries.

The armed forces wanted Japan to be strong. Generals and Admirals later took over the running of the government. They wanted to rid the Far East of American, British and European influence.

Why Japan began to Expand Overseas

People who wanted to emigrate to the USA were unable to do so because the American government restricted the numbers who could come.

Japan already had a colony on the mainland of Asia. In 1914 she had captured Germany's Chinese colonies but had had to give them back to China after the war. She felt she had a right to be in China.

SHANTUNG

KOREA

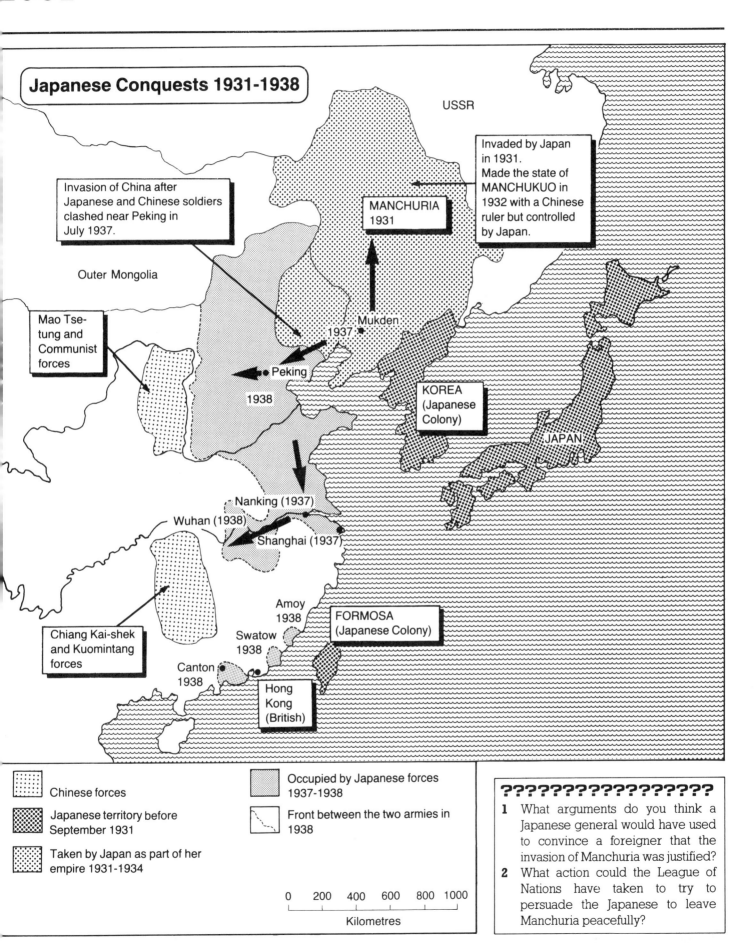

Japanese Conquests 1931-1938

USSR

Invaded by Japan in 1931.
Made the state of MANCHUKUO in 1932 with a Chinese ruler but controlled by Japan.

Invasion of China after Japanese and Chinese soldiers clashed near Peking in July 1937.

MANCHURIA 1931

Outer Mongolia

Mao Tse-tung and Communist forces

Mukden
1937

Peking
1938

KOREA (Japanese Colony)

JAPAN

Nanking (1937)

Wuhan (1938)

Shanghai (1937)

Chiang Kai-shek and Kuomintang forces

Amoy 1938

FORMOSA (Japanese Colony)

Swatow 1938

Canton 1938

Hong Kong (British)

Chinese forces

Japanese territory before September 1931

Taken by Japan as part of her empire 1931-1934

Occupied by Japanese forces 1937-1938

Front between the two armies in 1938

```
0    200   400   600   800  1000
```
Kilometres

???????????????????

1 What arguments do you think a Japanese general would have used to convince a foreigner that the invasion of Manchuria was justified?

2 What action could the League of Nations have taken to try to persuade the Japanese to leave Manchuria peacefully?

War in Abyssinia and Spain

War in Abyssinia (now called Ethiopia) in 1935-36, and the Spanish Civil War (1936-39) showed how weak the League of Nations really was. When the League tried to stop Mussolini in 1935, he only drew closer to Hitler. In 1936 he said 'The Berlin-Rome line is an axis around which the peaceful states of Europe can revolve.' This is why they were later known as the Axis Powers. In 1937 he joined Japan and Germany in signing the Anti-Comintern Pact against Communism. The links between Italy and Germany grew stronger when they both helped to supply weapons and soldiers to support General Franco's Nationalist forces, who rebelled against the Spanish government in 1936.

Why Mussolini invaded Abyssinia

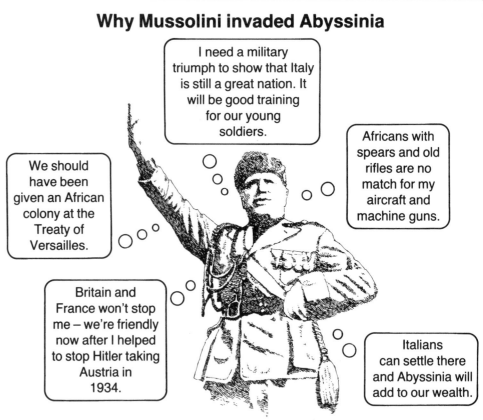

We should have been given an African colony at the Treaty of Versailles.

I need a military triumph to show that Italy is still a great nation. It will be good training for our young soldiers.

Africans with spears and old rifles are no match for my aircraft and machine guns.

Britain and France won't stop me – we're friendly now after I helped to stop Hitler taking Austria in 1934.

Italians can settle there and Abyssinia will add to our wealth.

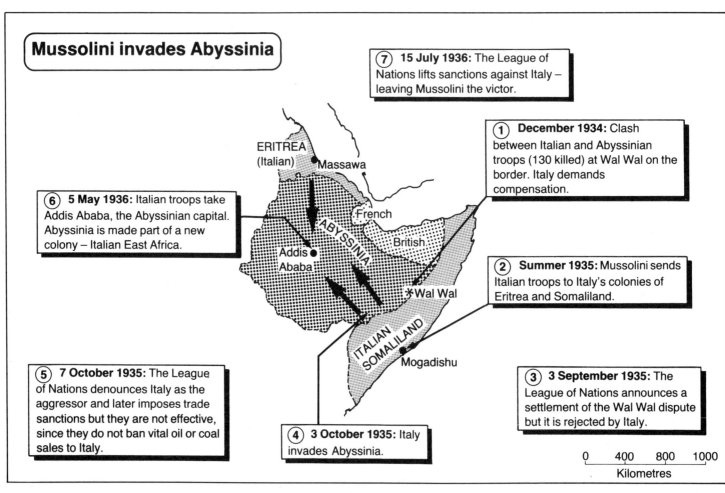

Mussolini invades Abyssinia

(7) **15 July 1936:** The League of Nations lifts sanctions against Italy – leaving Mussolini the victor.

(1) **December 1934:** Clash between Italian and Abyssinian troops (130 killed) at Wal Wal on the border. Italy demands compensation.

(6) **5 May 1936:** Italian troops take Addis Ababa, the Abyssinian capital. Abyssinia is made part of a new colony – Italian East Africa.

(2) **Summer 1935:** Mussolini sends Italian troops to Italy's colonies of Eritrea and Somaliland.

(5) **7 October 1935:** The League of Nations denounces Italy as the aggressor and later imposes trade sanctions but they are not effective, since they do not ban vital oil or coal sales to Italy.

(4) **3 October 1935:** Italy invades Abyssinia.

(3) **3 September 1935:** The League of Nations announces a settlement of the Wal Wal dispute but it is rejected by Italy.

ERITREA (Italian) — Massawa — French — British — ABYSSINIA — Addis Ababa — *Wal Wal — ITALIAN SOMALILAND — Mogadishu

0   400   800   1000
Kilometres

Time Line
The Spanish Civil War

Spring 1936 Spain is a Republic with a left-wing government, trying hard to control a country where murder and violence are increasing. When the government takes land from the rich and from the Catholic Church it stirs the army into action.

18 July 1936 Soldiers led by General Franco revolt in Spanish Morocco. At the same time other army units on the Spanish mainland rise up and join the campaign to overthrow the Republican government. Civil war has begun. The Nationalists, as Franco's Fascist supporters are called, have the backing of the Catholic Church and the landowners. The Republicans get most of their support from Communists, Socialists and workers in the large cities of Madrid and Barcelona.

December 1936 The League of Nations calls on other countries not to interfere in the Civil War and tries to stop weapons and soldiers reaching Spanish Ports.

1936-39 From 500,000 to 1,000,000 Spaniards die in the war. Both sides commit appalling atrocities; as many as 5000 priests may have been killed by the Republicans, whilst unarmed civilians perish in the Nationalists' bombing raids.

28 March 1939 Madrid surrenders and Franco's forces control the whole of Spain.

1939-1975 Franco rules Spain as a Fascist Dictator. The Spaniards call him the *Caudillo* (Leader).

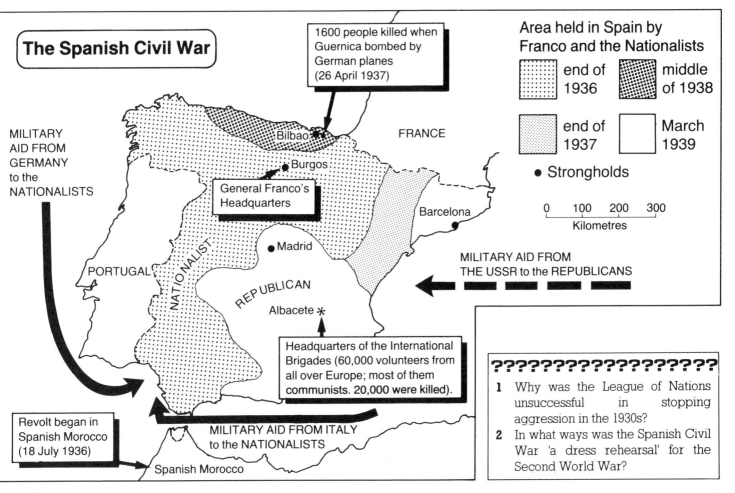

The Spanish Civil War

1600 people killed when Guernica bombed by German planes (26 April 1937)

Area held in Spain by Franco and the Nationalists

end of 1936

middle of 1938

end of 1937

March 1939

● Strongholds

0   100   200   300
Kilometres

MILITARY AID FROM GERMANY to the NATIONALISTS

FRANCE

Bilbao

Burgos

General Franco's Headquarters

Barcelona

NATIONALIST

● Madrid

PORTUGAL

REPUBLICAN

Albacete ✳

MILITARY AID FROM THE USSR to the REPUBLICANS

Headquarters of the International Brigades (60,000 volunteers from all over Europe; most of them communists. 20,000 were killed).

Revolt began in Spanish Morocco (18 July 1936)

MILITARY AID FROM ITALY to the NATIONALISTS

Spanish Morocco

???????????????????

1 Why was the League of Nations unsuccessful in stopping aggression in the 1930s?

2 In what ways was the Spanish Civil War 'a dress rehearsal' for the Second World War?

Steps to War 1936-39

One by one Hitler broke the terms of the Treaty of Versailles. In 1935 he reintroduced conscription (young people had to join the armed forces by law). Many people in Britain regarded the Treaty as being unfair to Germany; and when Hitler marched troops into the Rhineland (1936) they did not object, since it was his own country.

But by 1938 it was clear that Hitler's Germany was becoming more and more of a threat to peace in Europe. Hitler demanded *lebensraum* – living space for the German people. This was his excuse for invading other countries. In particular he wanted the boundaries of Germany to expand to include all those territories where the majority of the people were Germans or German-speaking.

This is why he forced Austria to agree to the *Anschluss* (union of the two German-speaking countries). He could later point to a plebiscite of the Austrian people to justify his actions, since 399 people in every 400 were said to have voted for Anschluss in April 1938. Many people in Europe were satisfied that this was what the Austrians really wanted, even if it did mean the persecution of Austria's Jews.

This policy of agreeing to Hitler's demands (in the vain hope that he would soon be satisfied) was called *appeasement*. It reached its climax with the Munich Peace Agreement on 29 September 1938. The desire for peace not war, was uppermost in people's minds. They still recalled with horror the senseless killing of the First World War. Britain, in particular, was not ready for war; she needed to rearm.

March 1936
Hitler marches troops into the Rhineland – forbidden by the Treaty of Versailles. Britain and France do nothing to stop him.

March 1938
Hitler forces Austria to join Germany in a union of the two countries (Anschluss) – forbidden by the Treaty of Versailles. German troops enter Austria. Britain and France do nothing to stop him.

October 1938
Hitler threatens to invade the German-speaking borderlands of Czechoslovakia (the Sudetenland) – a country formed by the Paris Peace Treaties in 1919. In September Britain and France prepare for war but eventually agree to let Germany have the Sudetenland in return for a promise of peace (The Munich Peace Agreement of 29 September, 1938).

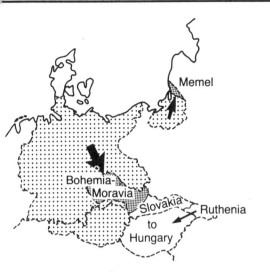

March 1939
Hitler annexes (takes) Bohemia – Moravia in Czechoslovakia – contrary to his promises at Munich. He also annexes Memel (part of Lithuania) – a German-speaking region which Germany lost at the Treaty of Versailles. At long last Britain and France realise no country in Europe is safe from Hitler's demands.

September 1939
Hitler invades Poland, having signed a pact with Russia not to attack one another. Britain and France declare war on Germany. The USSR invades Poland from the east and Germany and Russia divide Poland between them. The Second World War has begun.

Hitler's conquests in 18 months

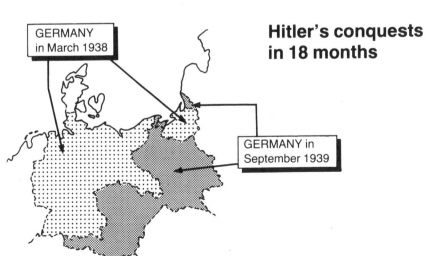

GERMANY in March 1938

GERMANY in September 1939

How the German Armed Forces Grew

1933   1939

The Army

🯅🯅🯅🯅🯅🯅🯅
7 DIVISIONS

Number of fully trained divisions ready for war

52 DIVISIONS

The Luftwaffe

Not allowed by the Treaty of Versailles
| 0 |

over 4000 planes

The Navy

Warships over 10,000 tonnes already launched

Not allowed by the Treaty of Versailles
| 0 |

| 4 |

Submarines

Not allowed by the Treaty of Versailles
| 0 |

| 54 |

??????????????????

1 At what point do *you think* Britain and France should have insisted that Germany keep to the terms agreed at the Treaty of Versailles?
2 Explain what was meant by appeasement.

Second World War: Germany goes to War

On 23 August 1939 Fascist Germany and Communist Russia signed a Non-Aggression Pact, promising not to go to war with one another. They secretly agreed to divide Poland and the Baltic Republics between them. Part of Poland (The Baltic Corridor) divided East Prussia from the rest of Germany, and this had annoyed the Germans ever since 1919. On 1 September 1939 German tanks, dive-bombers and a million soldiers made a swift and devastating attack (*Blitzkrieg*) on Poland. Britain and France had told Poland they would defend her frontiers from attack. Hitler thought they were bluffing and would not go to war; but he was wrong.

Time Line

1939

1 September	Hitler invades Poland.
3 September	Britain and France declare war on Germany.
17 September	Soviet Union invades Poland.
5 October	Poland is divided between Germany and the Soviet Union. Meanwhile Britain and France do nothing on land. For six months there is little action and people start to call it 'the Phoney War'. The Royal Navy patrols the seas and in December the Germans lose the battleship *Graf Spee* at the battle of the river Plate.

1940

9 April	Germany invades Norway and Denmark. Allied troops land near Narvik but are soon evacuated. Germany has won another swift victory.
10 May	Winston Churchill becomes British Prime Minister soon after the fall of Norway. On the same day Germany launches another *Blitzkrieg* – this time against Holland and Belgium.
14 May	Holland surrenders.
20 May	German tanks reach the Channel coast after slicing through the Allied defences. British troops are trapped.
28 May	Belgium surrenders.
27 May to 4 June	335,000 British and French troops are evacuated from Dunkirk. German armies begin the conquest of France.
10 June	Mussolini declares war on Britain and France.
14 June	Paris falls to German forces.
22 June	France agrees to an Armistice. The northern half of the country, including Paris, is now occupied by German forces. The southern half is unoccupied and governed by the French from the small town of Vichy (the 'Vichy Government').
July to October	The Battle of Britain. The Luftwaffe fails to destroy the Royal Air Force – the first step in the German invasion of England ('Operation Sea-lion'). Hitler has to call off the invasion. The *Blitz* (bombing of British cities) begins.
13 September	Italian troops invade Egypt.
9 December	British and Commonwealth forces win big victories against the Italians in North Africa and invade Libya (Italian colony).

1941

12 February	German reinforcements (Rommel's Afrika Corps) arrive in Libya to stem the British advance.
6 April	Axis troops invade Yugoslavia and Greece. Both surrender in just over a fortnight's fighting.
20 May	German airborne troops capture Crete after bitter fighting.

1939-41

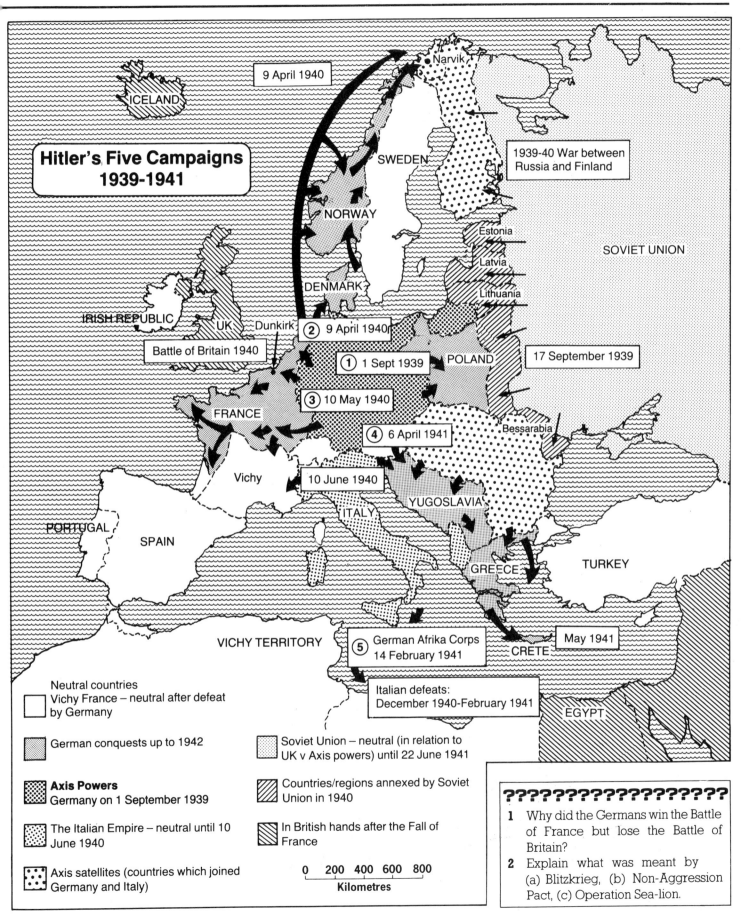

Hitler's Five Campaigns 1939-1941

9 April 1940

Narvik

ICELAND

SWEDEN

1939-40 War between Russia and Finland

NORWAY

SOVIET UNION

Estonia

Latvia

DENMARK

Lithuania

IRISH REPUBLIC

UK

Dunkirk

② 9 April 1940

Battle of Britain 1940

① 1 Sept 1939

POLAND

17 September 1939

③ 10 May 1940

FRANCE

④ 6 April 1941

Bessarabia

Vichy

10 June 1940

YUGOSLAVIA

PORTUGAL

ITALY

SPAIN

GREECE

TURKEY

VICHY TERRITORY

⑤ German Afrika Corps 14 February 1941

May 1941

CRETE

Italian defeats: December 1940-February 1941

EGYPT

Neutral countries
Vichy France – neutral after defeat by Germany

German conquests up to 1942

Soviet Union – neutral (in relation to UK v Axis powers) until 22 June 1941

Axis Powers
Germany on 1 September 1939

Countries/regions annexed by Soviet Union in 1940

The Italian Empire – neutral until 10 June 1940

In British hands after the Fall of France

Axis satellites (countries which joined Germany and Italy)

0 200 400 600 800
Kilometres

???????????????????

1 Why did the Germans win the Battle of France but lose the Battle of Britain?

2 Explain what was meant by (a) Blitzkrieg, (b) Non-Aggression Pact, (c) Operation Sea-lion.

35

Second World War: Operation Barbarossa

When Hitler abandoned plans to invade Britain in 1940, he turned his attention to the menace of Soviet Communism in the east. He wanted a large slice of Russia as part of his plan for a greater Germany. On 22 June 1941 he launched 'Operation Barbarossa', a massive invasion of the Soviet Union with a vast army, 8000 tanks and 3000 aircraft. It was his greatest mistake. The Soviet Union had a huge population, greater than that of all the Axis powers put together, vast resources to draw upon, an enormous land area, and a bitter winter climate.

Time Line

1941

22 June	'Operation Barbarossa' begins. Hitler invades the Soviet Union.
September	Fall of Kiev, one of the largest cities in the Soviet Union, together with 500,000 Russian troops killed, wounded or taken prisoner. German armies besiege Leningrad.
October	Moscow threatened. As the Russian armies retreat they burn crops and destroy materials and buildings which might be useful to the Germans. This is called a 'scorched earth' policy.
December	Marshal Zhukov begins a winter attack on German troops and forces them to retreat from Moscow.
7 December	Japanese attack on Pearl Harbor brings the United States into the war on the side of Britain and the Soviet Union. Convoys of arms and weapons are sent to help the Russians in their campaign against the Germans.

1942

May	After the long Russian winter, the German armies resume the offensive and push towards the Caucasus region where the main Russian oilfields are situated.
June	Rommel's Afrika Corps invades Egypt until halted at a place called El Alamein, about 300 kilometres from the Suez Canal. If this falls then Allied shipping will have to go the long way round (via South Africa), delaying vital supplies. Hitler could even go on to capture the Middle East oilfields and India.

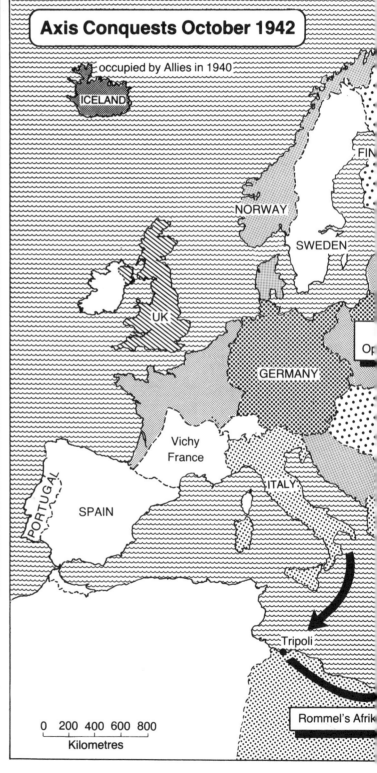

Axis Conquests October 1942

occupied by Allies in 1940

ICELAND

NORWAY

SWEDEN

FIN

UK

GERMANY

Op

Vichy France

PORTUGAL

SPAIN

ITALY

Tripoli

Rommel's Afrik

0 200 400 600 800
Kilometres

and the U-Boat War

The War in the Atlantic

Supplies of food and raw materials were vital to Britain during the Second World War. Many of these had to come by sea from North America and the Commonwealth. German submarines, called U-boats, attacked the merchant ships which carried these vital supplies. Hundreds of ships were torpedoed and sunk. Thousands of merchant seamen were drowned. Gradually the Royal Navy worked out ways of dealing with U-boats. Ships sailed in convoys, protected by destroyers armed with depth charges and submarine detectors. The graph shows when the Allies were losing the war in the Atlantic and when they won it.

Map legend:
- Germany
- Italian Empire
- Axis satellites
- German conquests up to 1942
- Russia
- UK or British Empire
- Occupied by Allies
- Neutral
- ★ German targets

U S S R

1941-42 LENINGRAD

October-December 1941 MOSCOW

November 1942-February 1943 STALINGRAD

barossa

CAUCASUS (OIL)

TURKEY

October 1942 EL ALAMEIN

oruk

SUEZ CANAL

Turning points in the war   1942

4 November Battle of El Alamein. Montgomery's Eighth Army defeats Rommel's Afrika Corps and drives them back towards the Libyan border.

8 November British and American troops land in Morocco and Algeria in the campaign called 'Operation Torch'. They drive eastwards towards Tunis.

19 November German forces, are caught in a trap as the Red Army encircles them at Stalingrad.

The U-Boat War

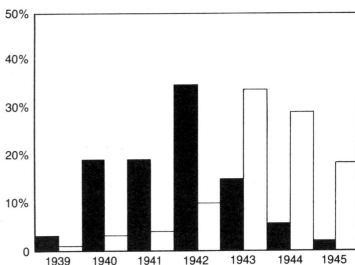

The columns show the % of total WW2 losses in each of the war years.

- ■ Allied shipping sunk
- □ German U-boats sunk

??????????????????????????

1   What was the importance of the battles of (a) Stalingrad, (b) El Alamein, (c) the Atlantic? Draw a small sketch map to illustrate each battle.

2   What did Hitler hope to gain by attacking British and Commonwealth forces in North Africa and by invading the Soviet Union?

Second World War: War Against Japan

On 7 December 1941 the Japanese launched a dramatic attack on the United States naval base of Pearl Harbor in Hawaii. Pearl Harbor is in the middle of the Pacific Ocean, and the powerful US Navy was the biggest threat to Japan in the area. The Japanese planners hoped to destroy the major US battleships and aircraft carriers as they lay at anchor.

They did not declare war in advance, so the Americans had no warning of the attack. Over 2,400 Americans were killed in the attack and a large number of planes were destroyed. Two battleships were sunk and the other six damaged, but the aircraft carriers were at sea and escaped. As a result the United States entered the war, determined to avenge Pearl Harbor.

Almost simultaneously the Japanese invaded other Allied territories in the Far East and sank two British battleships off the coast of Malaya.

Time Line

1941

7 December	Japanese attack on Pearl Harbor.
8 December	The United States and Britain declare war on Japan. Japanese invade Malaya.
10 December	HMS Prince of Wales and HMS Repulse are sunk by Japanese bombers off the coast of Malaya. Japanese troops seize the US island of Guam.
11 December	Japanese troops invade the Philippine Islands (US territory). Germany and Italy declare war on the United States.
25 December	Fall of Hong Kong.

1942

3 January	Japanese troops invade Borneo and the Dutch East Indies.
15 January	Japanese troops invade Burma.
15 February	Singapore surrenders to the Japanese.
7 March	Japanese troops invade New Guinea.
9 March	Java surrenders to the Japanese.
4-8 May	Battle of the Coral Sea halts further Japanese invasions in the South Pacific. Had the Japanese been successful, Australia and New Zealand would have been in danger.
6 May	Fall of the Philippine Islands to the Japanese.
20 May	Japanese victorious in Burma.
3-6 June	Battle of Midway. Four Japanese aircraft carriers sunk. This is the turning point in the war against Japan. From now on Japan is losing.
7 August	American troops land on Guadalcanal. The Americans attack the Japanese by 'hopping' from one Pacific island to another.

1943

20 November	American marines capture the island of Tarawa.

1944

21 July	American troops land on Guam.
20 October	American troops land on the Philippines.
23-24 October	Battle of Leyte Gulf. The Japanese Navy, heavily outnumbered, attacks the American fleet in the greatest naval battle in history – the Japanese lose 27 major warships, the Americans lose 6 warships.

1945

19 February to 26 March	American marines land on Iwo Jima. Six thousand are killed securing the island, so that it can become an air base.
1 April to 22 June	American troops land on Okinawa, only 500 kilometres from the Japanese mainland. Over 12,000 Americans and 100,000 Japanese are killed.
3 May	British and Commonwealth forces under Admiral Lord Mountbatten capture Rangoon, capital of Burma.
6 August	American aircraft *Enola Gay* drops atom bomb on Hiroshima. About 100,000 Japanese die eventually from the effects of the bomb. Allies hope the Japanese will surrender immediately. When this does not happen a second atom bomb is dropped on Nagasaki.
14 August	Japan surrenders. The war is over.

???

1 What did the Japanese hope to gain by attacking Pearl Harbor? How were they trying to expand their Empire?

2 Why was Pearl Harbor a turning point in the war against Germany and Italy?

3 Write down arguments for and against the dropping of the atom bombs on Japan.

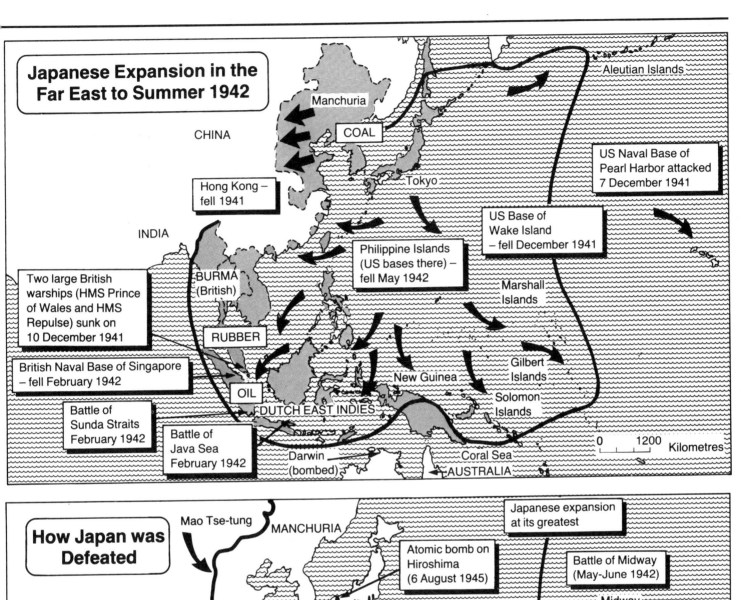

Japanese Expansion in the Far East to Summer 1942

Manchuria

CHINA

COAL

Tokyo

Hong Kong – fell 1941

INDIA

US Naval Base of Pearl Harbor attacked 7 December 1941

US Base of Wake Island – fell December 1941

Philippine Islands (US bases there) – fell May 1942

BURMA (British)

Marshall Islands

Two large British warships (HMS Prince of Wales and HMS Repulse) sunk on 10 December 1941

RUBBER

British Naval Base of Singapore – fell February 1942

OIL

New Guinea

Gilbert Islands

Solomon Islands

Battle of Sunda Straits February 1942

DUTCH EAST INDIES

Battle of Java Sea February 1942

Darwin (bombed)

Coral Sea

AUSTRALIA

Aleutian Islands

0   1200   Kilometres

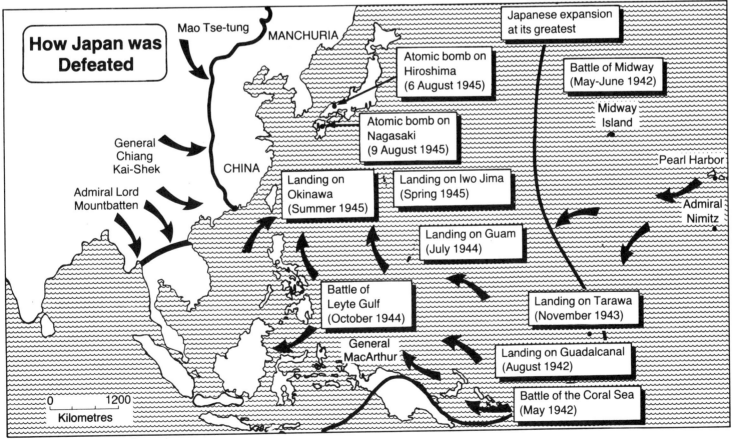

How Japan was Defeated

Mao Tse-tung   MANCHURIA

Japanese expansion at its greatest

Atomic bomb on Hiroshima (6 August 1945)

Battle of Midway (May-June 1942)

Midway Island

General Chiang Kai-Shek

CHINA

Atomic bomb on Nagasaki (9 August 1945)

Pearl Harbor

Admiral Lord Mountbatten

Landing on Okinawa (Summer 1945)

Landing on Iwo Jima (Spring 1945)

Admiral Nimitz

Landing on Guam (July 1944)

Battle of Leyte Gulf (October 1944)

Landing on Tarawa (November 1943)

General MacArthur

Landing on Guadalcanal (August 1942)

Battle of the Coral Sea (May 1942)

0   1200   Kilometres

Second World War: Victory in Europe

Time Line

1943

14 January The siege of Leningrad ends when Russian armies come to the rescue.

31 January The German Sixth Army surrenders at Stalingrad.

13 May The end of the war in North Africa. Over 200,000 German and Italian soldiers are captured in Tunisia.

5 July The Germans and the Russians fight the biggest tank battle in history at Kursk. Over two million men are involved, together with 6000 tanks and 30,000 guns. The Russians succeed in pushing the Germans back; and continue to move forward for the rest of the war.

10 July Allied forces invade Sicily.

25 July Mussolini is deposed in Italy. He is replaced by Marshal Badoglio.

7 August Allied planes bomb Peenemunde, where Hitler's scientists are working on new missiles, called the V-1 and V-2.

3 September The Allies invade Italy.

8 September Italy surrenders; but the Germans rush troops into Italy to stop the Allies advancing.

10 September German troops occupy Rome.

13 October Italy declares war on Germany.

6 November The Red Army takes Kiev.

1944

22 January Allied forces land at Anzio in Italy.

29 January – 30 May German forces pin the Allies down at Cassino in Italy.

4 June The Allies take Rome.

5 June French Resistance workers are warned that D-Day is imminent. These Partisans, like those in Yugoslavia, perform many courageous acts behind enemy lines, such as sabotaging bridges and railways.

6 June D-Day. The largest invasion in history. A huge armada of 5000 ships lands 150,000 soldiers and 6000 tanks and armoured vehicles in Normandy, north France.

13 June Germans launch V-1 missiles ('Flying bombs') at south-eastern England. They are too late to have an effect on the war.

1 August The Warsaw Uprisings – Poles, thinking the Russians are on their way to help them, rise up against the Germans. The revolt is brutally put down. The Russians do not come.

15 August Allied landings in southern France.

25 August Paris is freed. Finland makes peace with Russia.

3 September Brussels is freed.

16 September Bulgaria makes peace and later declares war on Germany. Germany fires V-2 rockets at south-eastern England.

29 October Russians reach Budapest in Hungary.

16 December Battle of the Bulge – German forces counter-attack in Belgium but are beaten off.

1945

12 January Germans in retreat on every front.

17 January Russians take Warsaw.

13 February Russians take Budapest.

7 March Allies cross the Rhine. They invade Germany for the first time in the war.

13 April Russians take Vienna.

25 April American and Russian troops meet at Torgau.

29 April Mussolini is killed by Italian partisans.

30 April Hitler commits suicide in Berlin.

2 May The Russians take Berlin. The German army in Italy surrenders.

8 May VE Day (Victory in Europe): Germany surrenders.

In the summer of 1942 the Axis powers suffered serious defeats for the first time. In May and June 1942 the American Navy won big victories in the Coral Sea and at Midway. In August 1942 American marines landed on Guadalcanal. In November the British Eighth Army won a decisive victory at El Alamein in Egypt; and on 31 January 1943 the German Sixth Army surrendered to the Russians at Stalingrad. The Allies were on the attack.

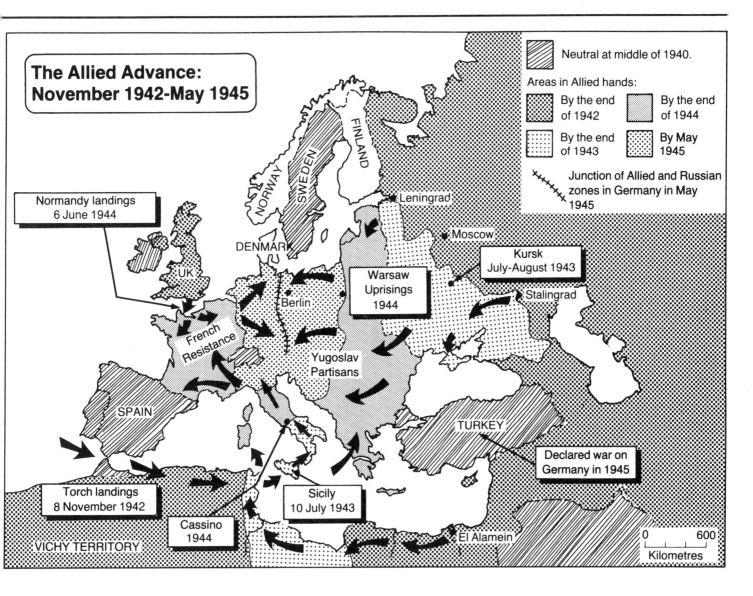

The Allied Advance: November 1942–May 1945

Neutral at middle of 1940.

Areas in Allied hands:
By the end of 1942
By the end of 1944
By the end of 1943
By May 1945

Junction of Allied and Russian zones in Germany in May 1945

Normandy landings 6 June 1944

NORWAY
SWEDEN
FINLAND
DENMARK
UK
Leningrad
Moscow
Warsaw Uprisings 1944
Kursk July–August 1943
Stalingrad
Berlin
French Resistance
Yugoslav Partisans
SPAIN
TURKEY
Declared war on Germany in 1945
Torch landings 8 November 1942
Sicily 10 July 1943
Cassino 1944
VICHY TERRITORY
El Alamein

0   600
Kilometres

Numbers of People Killed in the Second World War

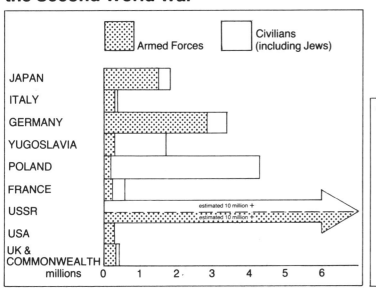

Armed Forces   Civilians (including Jews)

JAPAN
ITALY
GERMANY
YUGOSLAVIA
POLAND
FRANCE
USSR — estimated 10 million +
estimated 10 million +
USA
UK & COMMONWEALTH

millions   0   1   2   3   4   5   6

?????????????????????????????

1 Which battles were the main turning points for the Allies in the Second World War?

2 Who suffered most and who benefitted most from Germany's defeat in 1945?

3 Stalin wanted the Allies to invade Europe in 1943 – a year before the eventual D-Day in June 1944. What were the advantages and disadvantages to Russia and to the Allies of such a plan? Find out how an earlier invasion might have affected the boundaries of countries in Europe after the war.

The Cold War: Europe in 1945

Whilst the Allies were still at war with the Axis powers they gave a lot of thought to what should be done when the war ended. Three conferences were held at Teheran in 1943, Yalta in 1945 (February) and at Potsdam after the war ended.

Some of the Allies did not trust the Russians; nor did the Russians trust the Allies. Stalin knew that many western leaders were bitterly opposed to communism. He wanted to push the frontiers of the Soviet Union as far as possible and he did this by annexing (taking) part of Poland into Russia (as agreed at the Yalta conference) and by making sure that most countries freed by the Russian Red Army had Communist governments dependent on the USSR.

LEADERS	PLACE	TIME	WHAT WAS AGREED
			(apart from matters concerning the immediate conduct of the war)
Stalin Roosevelt Churchill	Teheran (Iran)	Autumn 1943	Set up the United Nations as soon as the war ended.
Stalin Roosevelt Churchill	Yalta (USSR)	Spring 1945	Some territorial changes to Poland and the Soviet Union after the war; free elections in countries freed by the Allies.
Stalin Truman Churchill & Attlee	Potsdam (Germany)	Summer 1945	Divided Germany into 4 occupation zones – USA, USSR, UK, France. Discussed how Germany should be governed. Already some serious disagreements with Russia.

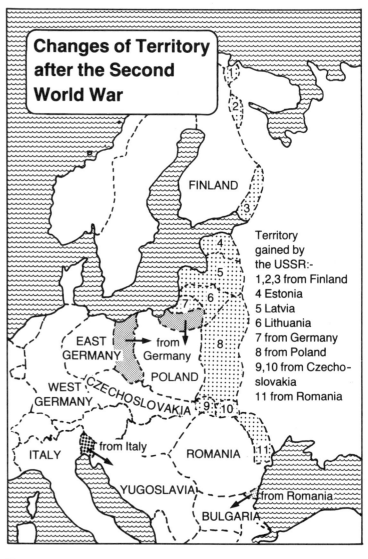

Changes of Territory after the Second World War

Territory gained by the USSR:-
1,2,3 from Finland
4 Estonia
5 Latvia
6 Lithuania
7 from Germany
8 from Poland
9,10 from Czechoslovakia
11 from Romania

Landmarks of the Cold War

The Iron Curtain
Winston Churchill in a speech at Fulton, Missouri, USA.
5 March 1946
'From Stettin in the Baltic to Trieste in the Adriatic an *iron curtain* has descended across the Continent.'

The Truman Doctrine
Harry S. Truman, US President to Congress.
12 March 1947
'I believe that it must be the policy of the United States to support free peoples who are resisting attempted subjugation by armed minorities or by outside pressures.'

The Marshall Plan
June 1947
The Americans agreed to provide financial aid to help the countries of Western Europe recover from the war. It was called Marshall Aid after the US Secretary of State, George Marshall, who invented the scheme.

The Berlin Blockade
June 1948 to May 1949

The Western Allies made plans to merge the three western Occupation Zones into one country – West Germany – but West Berlin remained as an island in the middle of the Russian Zone. Stalin found this intolerable; so on 23 June 1948 Russian troops closed all the road, rail and canal routes into West Berlin from West Germany, hoping to starve West Berlin of food and raw materials and force it to become part of East Germany.

The Allies replied by flying in everything West Berlin needed. Planes took off night and day for nearly eleven months. By May 1949 the Russians realised they could not win and lifted the Blockade. The dispute made sure there would now be two Germanies and two Berlins.

NATO (North Atlantic Treaty Organisation)
4 April 1949

'The Parties agree that an armed attack against one or more of them in Europe or North America shall be considered an attack against them all'

This was the main part of the North Atlantic Treaty which started a new military alliance of West against East. It directly involved the United States in defending western Europe, and like Marshall Aid and the Truman Doctrine, was the end to the old American policy of Isolationism.

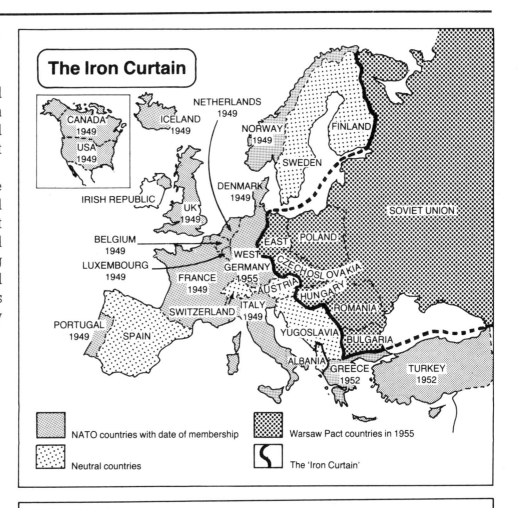

The Iron Curtain

NATO countries with date of membership

Neutral countries

Warsaw Pact countries in 1955

The 'Iron Curtain'

Occupation Zones Immediately After the Second World War

now part of Poland

Berlin and Vienna were each divided into four occupation zones.

???????????????????

1 Explain how each of the following came into being (a) the Cold War, (b) the division of Germany into East and West, (c) NATO.
2 How and why was Berlin blockaded? How did the Western Allies defeat the Blockade?

43

The United Nations

Over the years the United Nations has had many successes and many failures. Peace-keeping forces have been sent to several of the world's troublespots but the big powers have often stopped the UN from acting in areas where they have an interest. The UN did not manage to stop the fighting between the USA and North Vietnam, or stop the USSR from invading Hungary and Afghanistan, or stop the 1971-72 war between India and Pakistan, or prevent the war between the UK and Argentina over the Falkland Islands.

Time Line

1943 The Allies agree to set up the United Nations when the war ends.

1944 Proposals for the UN Charter are prepared at the Dumbarton Oaks Conference (USA).

1945 Fifty nations sign the charter at the San Francisco Conference. On October 24 the United Nations comes into existence. Its aims are PEACE, HUMAN RIGHTS, EQUALITY, ELIMINATION OF POVERTY, IMPROVED LIVING STANDARDS. The UN sets up specialised agencies such as WHO (health) and UNESCO (education).

?????????????????????????

1 How, why and when was the United Nations founded? What part does (a) the Security Council (b) the General Assembly play in its work?

2 In what ways has the United Nations been more or less successful than the League of Nations?

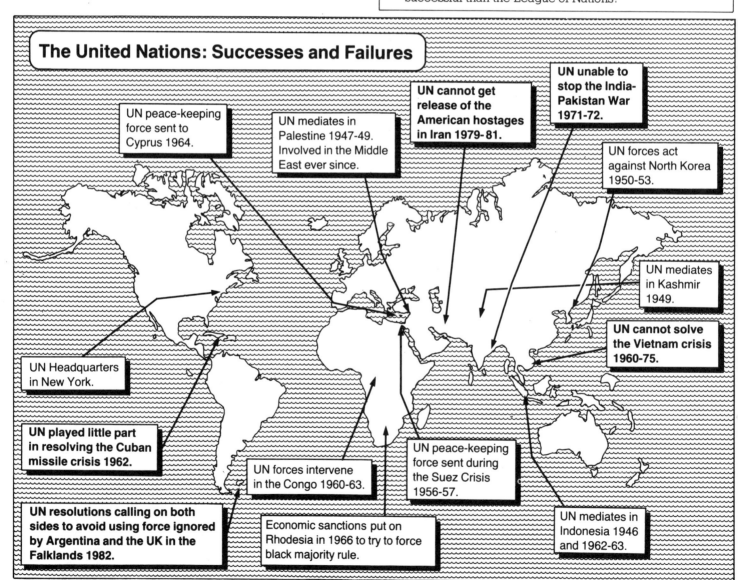

The United Nations: Successes and Failures

UN peace-keeping force sent to Cyprus 1964.

UN mediates in Palestine 1947-49. Involved in the Middle East ever since.

UN cannot get release of the American hostages in Iran 1979-81.

UN unable to stop the India-Pakistan War 1971-72.

UN forces act against North Korea 1950-53.

UN mediates in Kashmir 1949.

UN cannot solve the Vietnam crisis 1960-75.

UN Headquarters in New York.

UN played little part in resolving the Cuban missile crisis 1962.

UN forces intervene in the Congo 1960-63.

UN peace-keeping force sent during the Suez Crisis 1956-57.

UN mediates in Indonesia 1946 and 1962-63.

UN resolutions calling on both sides to avoid using force ignored by Argentina and the UK in the Falklands 1982.

Economic sanctions put on Rhodesia in 1966 to try to force black majority rule.

Some of the UN's Agencies

Specialised Agencies of the United Nations		Aims
FAO	Food and Agriculture Organisation	To improve farming methods, increase food production, eliminate famine.
WHO	World Health Organisation	Raise health standards, eliminate killer diseases, control epidemics.
UNESCO	United Nations Educational Scientific and Cultural Organisation	To raise educational standards, promote human rights and the rule of law.
ILO	International Labour Organisation	Improve working conditions and raise living standards.
GATT	General Agreement on Tariffs and Trade	Make it easier for goods to be traded between countries.
IMF	International Monetary Fund	To prevent extremes in the exchange rate – making it easier to exchange one country's money for another.
WORLD BANK		Provide loans for building projects benefitting peoples (e.g. dams).
UNICEF	United Nations Children's Fund	Help the world's children.

The Main Bodies of the United Nations

① GENERAL ASSEMBLY

DEBATES WORLD PROBLEMS

154 NATIONS

* each member country has one vote
* motions require a two-thirds majority if important
* otherwise a simple majority of YES votes over NO votes

② SECURITY COUNCIL

USSR   USA   UK
FRANCE   CHINA
5 Permanent Members

TAKES IMMEDIATE ACTION ON BEHALF OF THE UN AS A WHOLE

10 Elected Members (2 years only)

* each member has one vote
* successful motions require at least 9 YES votes and no NO votes from the five permanent members of the council

③ THE SECRETARIAT
(New York, USA)

RUNS THE UN

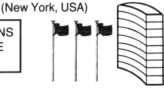

UN is run by a Secretary-General with the help of a large staff of officials appointed from the different member countries

④ THE TRUSTEESHIP COUNCIL

IN CHARGE OF TERRITORIES UNDER UN CONTROL OR MANDATE

USSR   CHINA   FRANCE   UK   USA

⑤ THE ECONOMIC AND SOCIAL COUNCIL

OVERSEES MATTERS RELATING TO HEALTH, EDUCATION ETC. SUPERVISES THE WORK OF THE SPECIALISED AGENCIES OF THE UN.

elected by the General Assembly

⑥ INTERNATIONAL COURT OF JUSTICE
(The Hague, Netherlands)

SETTLES LEGAL DISPUTES BETWEEN COUNTRIES

One judge from each of fifteen countries (9 years in office)

India and Pakistan

In 1946 India was the second most populated country in the world with over 400 million people; but she was still part of the British Empire. The Indians wanted to be free.

In 1919, 379 people had been killed when British troops fired on a peaceful demonstration in Amritsar. This made millions of Indians very angry. Gandhi, Nehru and other leaders of the Indian National Congress Party started organising many protest meetings and demonstrations to try to make the British give India independence.

In 1935 the Government of India Act gave the provinces of India their own governments but it still did not grant India its independence. As most of the provincial governments were then controlled by Hindus, the Moslems, (led by Mohammed Ali Jinnah) demanded self-government in a new state of Pakistan if India became independent. The Second World War made Britain put off giving them independence; so the Congress Party began a 'Quit India' campaign against the British.

Time Line

1946 Britain's Labour government tries to get the Hindus and Moslems to agree to a constitution without dividing the country into two. But talks break down and there are serious riots; over 4000 people are killed in Calcutta in clashes between Hindus and Moslems.

1947 In February Britain announces that, come what may, India will become independent by the middle of 1948. Lord Mountbatten is made Viceroy. India's turmoil soon convinces him that Britain must grant independence immediately. India is divided (partitioned) into three parts with the North West and part of the Punjab becoming West Pakistan, and part of Bengal in the North East becoming East Pakistan. Both Pakistans are separated by over 1600 kilometres of India which makes things very difficult for Pakistan.

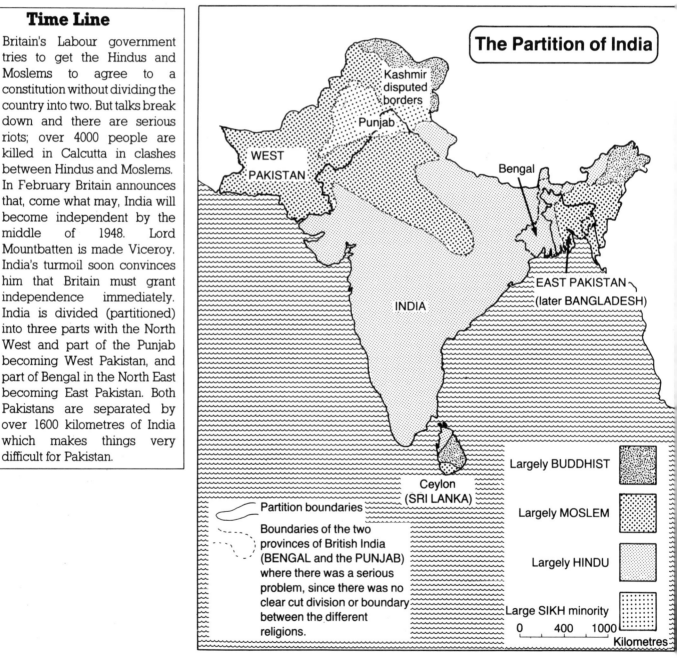

The Partition of India

Kashmir disputed borders

Punjab

WEST PAKISTAN

Bengal

INDIA

EAST PAKISTAN (later BANGLADESH)

Ceylon (SRI LANKA)

Partition boundaries

Boundaries of the two provinces of British India (BENGAL and the PUNJAB) where there was a serious problem, since there was no clear cut division or boundary between the different religions.

Largely BUDDHIST

Largely MOSLEM

Largely HINDU

Large SIKH minority

0   400   1000

Kilometres

After Partition

India and Pakistan fought over Kashmir in 1948 and 1965. The Hindu ruler wanted Kashmir to become part of India, but many of the Kashmir people were Moslem and wanted to join Pakistan.

India remained a democracy led by Nehru from 1947 to 1964, and by his daughter, Mrs Indira Gandhi, from 1966 to 1977, and 1980 onwards. Pakistan had a series of military governments. In 1971 there was a row between the largest political parties in East and West Pakistan. East Pakistan broke away and claimed independence as Bangladesh. Civil war broke out and millions of refugees fled across the border into India. India eventually declared war on Pakistan, forcing them to surrender. Bangladesh became an independent state.

Time Line

1947 Partition means that many Hindus now live in Moslem Pakistan and many Moslems live in Hindu India. Violence erupts. Brutal massacres on one side or other lead to the flight of refugees across the border with tales of the killings. These lead to further killings in retaliation. In the end over half a million Hindus, Sikhs and Moslems are massacred. The Indians have paid a terrible price for their independence.

1948 Mahatma Gandhi appeals for calm but is himself assassinated by a fanatical Hindu.

?????????????????????????

1 Explain why and how an independent India and Pakistan came to be formed in 1947. Was partition the best solution?

2 Have events since 1947 justified the decision to partition India?

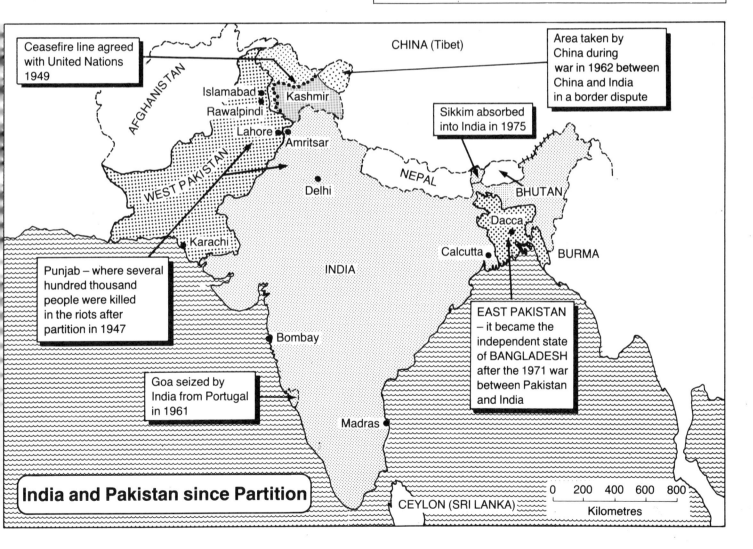

India and Pakistan since Partition

Ceasefire line agreed with United Nations 1949

Area taken by China during war in 1962 between China and India in a border dispute

Sikkim absorbed into India in 1975

Punjab – where several hundred thousand people were killed in the riots after partition in 1947

EAST PAKISTAN – it became the independent state of BANGLADESH after the 1971 war between Pakistan and India

Goa seized by India from Portugal in 1961

CHINA (Tibet)

AFGHANISTAN

Islamabad
Rawalpindi
Kashmir
Lahore
Amritsar
WEST PAKISTAN
Delhi
Karachi
INDIA
Bombay
Madras

NEPAL
BHUTAN
Dacca
Calcutta
BURMA

CEYLON (SRI LANKA)

0 200 400 600 800
Kilometres

The Chinese Revolution

Diary of the Chinese Revolution

1 1934-35: Mao Tse-tung successfully leads the Red Army on the Long March from southern China to the Yenan area, their new base.

2 1936-37: The Communists and Chiang Kai-shek's Kuomintang (Nationalists) agree a truce and jointly fight Japan when she invades China in 1937.

4

3 1937-45: The Chinese-Japanese War becomes a world war but the Nationalists often seem more interested in beating the Communists than throwing the Japanese out of China.

August 1945: Japan surrenders after the dropping of the Atomic Bombs, even though she holds a large part of China. The Communists and the Kuomintang fight to see who should control the Japanese-held territory.

5 1945-46

The Communists control the countryside but the Kuomintang hold most of the important cities. They are helped by the Americans. Mao Tse-tung believes that a Communist Revolution will only succeed if the peasants are on his side. He promises a fair share of the land to the peasants and relief from poverty. His troops make friends with the peasants – unlike the Kuomintang who treat them badly and often take their food and property. Mao Tse-tung and his generals prove to be skilful leaders and experts at guerilla warfare; the Kuomintang army, however, is riddled with corruption (people taking bribes) and its leaders are inefficient.

6 1946-48: Civil war breaks out and the Communists harass the Kuomintang forces who are very much larger in number. Gradually the Red Armies take over much of Manchuria and northern China.

Taiwan

7 1948-49: The Communists win a decisive battle at Huai-Hai and go on to take Peking, Nanking and Shanghai. China becomes the People's Republic (October 1949) and the Nationalists escape to Taiwan.

Landmarks of the Chinese Revolution since 1949

1950-56 China had been devastated by the war against Japan. So Mao had to develop heavy industry to rebuild China. Land was taken from the rich landowners and given to the peasants. Later it was organised into collective farms. Hospitals, schools and clinics were opened.

1957 Mao Tse-tung called for open public discussion: 'Let a hundred flowers blossom and a hundred schools of thought compete' – but it was abandoned when too many people took advantage of it and criticised the government.

1958 **The Great Leap Forward** – huge communes were formed by merging the collective farms together. People were encouraged to set up workshops and even backyard iron furnaces to produce the goods and raw materials China needed.

1960 Relations with the Soviet Union began to get worse and there were disputes along the Russian-Chinese border.

1965-69 **The Cultural Revolution** – Mao wanted to rekindle the revolutionary spirit. Young people organised themselves as Red Guards and denounced people who they thought were not true communists. Great emphasis was placed on manual labour, rather than on expert advice. Peasants were trained to perform simple medical tasks and sent out to work on the communes as 'barefoot doctors'.

1971 China was admitted as a member of the United Nations in place of Nationalist China (Taiwan). Relations with the United States began to improve – China wanted an ally against the Soviet Union.

1976 Mao Tse-tung and Chou En-lai died. Mao's successors clamped down on the Cultural Revolution and put Mao's widow and the other members of the 'Gang of Four' on trial and accused them of abusing their positions of power. Relations with the western world rapidly improved.

Growth in Production – 1950-1980					
1950		**1980**			
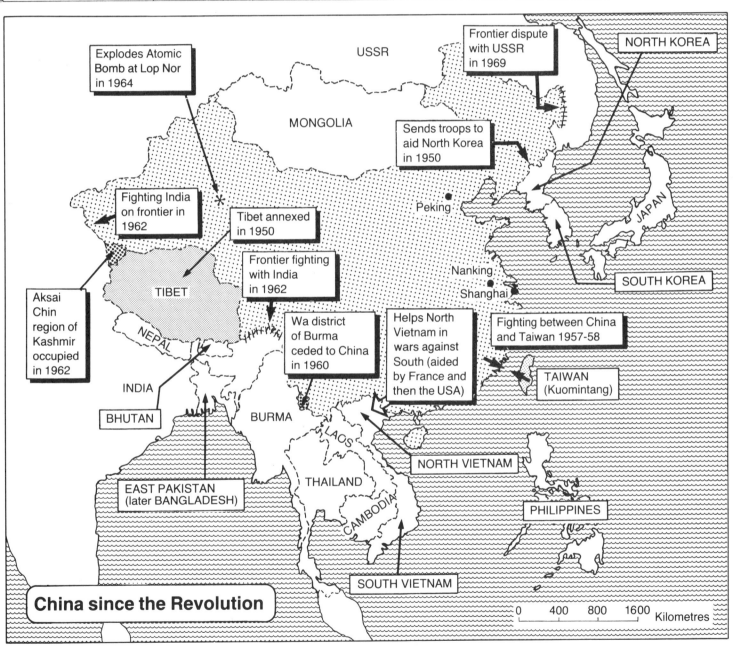 32 million tonnes	COAL	🐾🐾🐾🐾🐾🐾🐾🐾🐾🐾🐾🐾🐾🐾🐾🐾🐾	500 million tonnes	= 30 million tonnes	
hardly any	OIL	🛢🛢🛢🛢🛢🛢🛢🛢🛢🛢	100 million tonnes	= 10 million tonnes	
hardly any	STEEL	◢◢◢◢◢◢◢◢	35 million tonnes	= 5 million tonnes	
hardly any	ELECTRICITY	ϞϞϞϞϞϞϞϞϞϞϞϞϞϞ	280 billion kWh	= 20 billion kWh	
120 million tonnes	RICE, WHEAT MAIZE (GRAIN)	🌾🌾🌾🌾🌾🌾🌾🌾🌾🌾🌾	330 million tonnes	= 30 million tonnes	

China since the Revolution

Labels on map:
- Explodes Atomic Bomb at Lop Nor in 1964
- Frontier dispute with USSR in 1969
- NORTH KOREA
- USSR
- MONGOLIA
- Sends troops to aid North Korea in 1950
- Peking
- JAPAN
- Fighting India on frontier in 1962
- Tibet annexed in 1950
- Frontier fighting with India in 1962
- Nanking
- Shanghai
- SOUTH KOREA
- Aksai Chin region of Kashmir occupied in 1962
- TIBET
- NEPAL
- Wa district of Burma ceded to China in 1960
- Helps North Vietnam in wars against South (aided by France and then the USA)
- Fighting between China and Taiwan 1957-58
- TAIWAN (Kuomintang)
- INDIA
- BHUTAN
- BURMA
- LAOS
- NORTH VIETNAM
- EAST PAKISTAN (later BANGLADESH)
- THAILAND
- CAMBODIA
- PHILIPPINES
- SOUTH VIETNAM
- 0 400 800 1600 Kilometres

??

1 Describe the main steps by which Mao Tse-tung was able to defeat the Nationalists and establish Communist Party rule in China.

2 What advantages has communism given China? Can you see any disadvantages?

The Korean War

Korea had been Japanese since 1910. But during the Second World War the Allies promised that it would become independent when the fighting ended. In 1945 it was divided into two zones marked by the 38th parallel (38° North), to allow the Japanese forces to surrender to the Soviet army in the northern zone, and to the American army in the south. As in Germany, efforts to reunite the two zones failed; so in 1948 both zones became independent republics and the Russian and American forces returned home. A year later fighting broke out.

Time Line

25 June 1950 North Korean armies suddenly cross the border and invade South Korea. They sweep southwards, capturing Seoul the capital city, and hem in the South Korean army in the south east near Pusan. The Security Council at the United Nations demands the withdrawal of the North Korean forces. The UN later decides to send troops to Korea. These are placed under the command of the American General, Douglas MacArthur.

15 September 1950 MacArthur makes a brilliant start to his campaign to recapture South Korea by landing troops at Inchon, retaking Seoul and linking up with soldiers who have broken out of the Pusan perimeter zone.

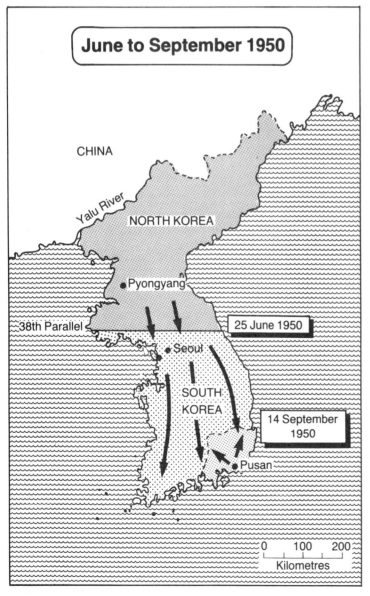

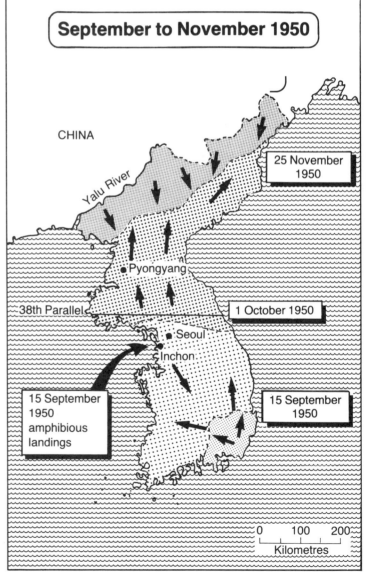

Time Line

October–November 1950   MacArthur's forces drive the enemy back into North Korea. The Chinese threaten to intervene if the Americans cross the 38th parallel. The US and UN now intend to reunite the two Koreas.

26 November 1950   China enters the war and huge armies drive the UN forces back into South Korea. MacArthur wishes to carry the war into China by bombing air bases and even threatening to use the Atom Bomb. But

Truman has no desire to start a possible world war; so he sacks MacArthur.

8 July 1951   The two opposing forces reach stalemate and face each other across a front line which is virtually the same when peace is finally agreed in 1953. So the United Nations' forces successfully repel the aggressor but at a terrible loss of life and the virtual destruction of much of Korea.

Facts

★ Fifteen UN members sent troops, including Britain, Turkey and Canada.

★ The vast majority of the UN forces were from the USA and South Korea.

★ Over 54,000 American and 70,000 South Korean soldiers were killed, and a much larger number of Chinese and North Korean soldiers.

★ Gravest casualties, as in most wars, were among civilians – an estimated *three to four million* Koreans are believed to have died as a result of the fighting.

?????????????????????????

1 What led to the outbreak of war in Korea in 1950?
2 How and why did the United Nations and China become involved in the Korean War and with what results?

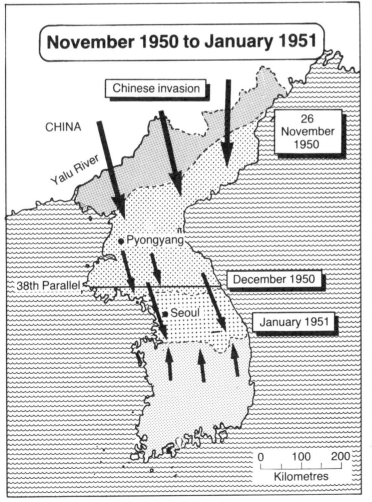

November 1950 to January 1951

Chinese invasion

CHINA

Yalu River

26 November 1950

Pyongyang

38th Parallel

December 1950

Seoul

January 1951

0   100   200
Kilometres

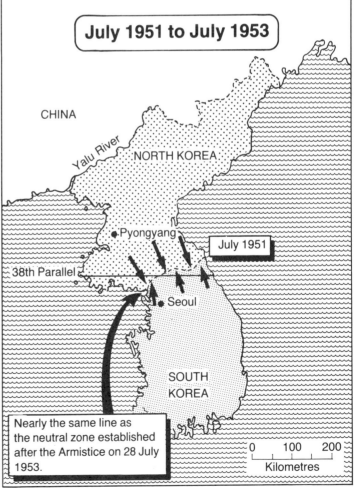

July 1951 to July 1953

CHINA

Yalu River

NORTH KOREA

Pyongyang

July 1951

38th Parallel

Seoul

SOUTH KOREA

Nearly the same line as the neutral zone established after the Armistice on 28 July 1953.

0   100   200
Kilometres

The Soviet Union after Stalin

Only four leaders had supreme control of this vast and powerful country in the entire period from 1917 to 1982. They were LENIN (1917-24), STALIN (1924-53), KHRUSCHEV (1953-64) and BREZHNEV (1964-82). The first two were dictators, the last two were members of the collective leadership of the Soviet Union. In the same period Britain had 14 different prime ministers, there were 13 different American presidents and about 75 separate French governments!

Khruschev

Stalin kept his grip on Russia, up to the time of his death in 1953, with the help of the secret police. Then Nikita Khruschev became first secretary of the Communist Party (the post Stalin held in 1923). Other leaders also sought the top job in the Soviet Union but Khruschev managed to demote them. He even sent Malenkov (Prime Minister after Stalin's death) away to manage a power station!

In 1956 Khruschev denounced Stalin at the 20th Party Congress, accusing him of many crimes, particularly those committed by the secret police and during the Purges before the war. Some Russian leaders (the hardliners) still believed in the Cold War but Khruschev believed in

peaceful co-existence. Although Khruschev worked for peace he could be just as tough as Stalin. He clamped down brutally on the Hungarians who rebelled in 1956 and he supported East Germany when they built the Berlin Wall in 1961. But he fell from power in 1964, mainly because he failed to solve Russia's economic problems. He had been responsible for a bold project to raise food production by farming the virgin lands of Kazakhstan. In fact wheat production rose by 50% in ten years but there were huge crop failures when drought hit the area in the 1960s.

In 1964 Khruschev was pushed out of office and succeeded by Leonid Brezhnev. There were no executions but neither were there any elections.

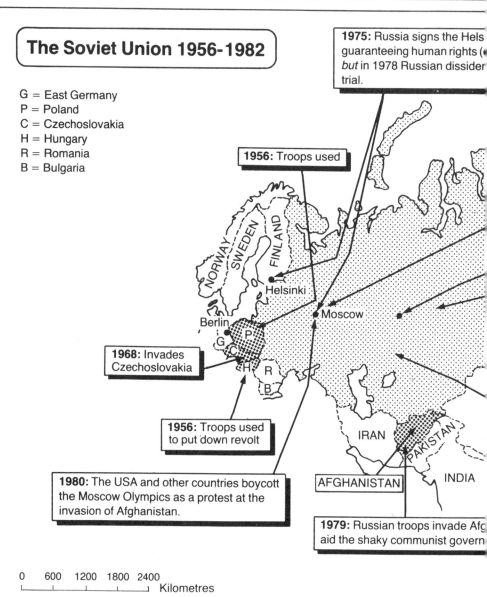

The Soviet Union 1956-1982

G = East Germany
P = Poland
C = Czechoslovakia
H = Hungary
R = Romania
B = Bulgaria

1956: Troops used

1968: Invades Czechoslovakia

1956: Troops used to put down revolt

1980: The USA and other countries boycott the Moscow Olympics as a protest at the invasion of Afghanistan.

1975: Russia signs the Hels guaranteeing human rights (*but* in 1978 Russian dissider trial.

1979: Russian troops invade Afg aid the shaky communist govern

AFGHANISTAN   INDIA

IRAN   PAKISTAN

NORWAY SWEDEN FINLAND

Helsinki

Berlin Moscow

G P
C
H R
B

0   600   1200 1800 2400
Kilometres

Annual Production i

1928 STALIN 1953 KHRUSCH

1928		1953
36 m		260 million

1928	1953	
4 m	27 million	STE

	1928	1953
	about 70 million	about 90 million

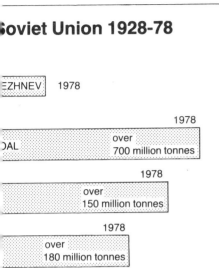

Soviet Union 1928-78

EZHNEV	1978

1978

OAL — over 700 million tonnes

1978

over 150 million tonnes

1978

over 180 million tonnes

Brezhnev

Leonid Brezhnev also believed in peaceful co-existence and worked to relax tension between east and west (détente). But he also believed Khruschev had gone too far in permitting criticism. Brezhnev cracked down hard on people in Russia who expressed opposition to the regime (the dissidents). By Western standards the punishments (imprisonment, labour camps) were harsh; by Stalin's standards they were extremely lenient. In 1968 Soviet troops joined with other Warsaw Pact countries to re-impose a stricter form of communism in Czechoslovakia and in 1979 Russian troops invaded Afghanistan to prevent the collapse of its communist government. Brezhnev died in 1982.

In the period since Stalin's death the Soviet Union developed new freedoms, a higher standard of living and the status of a superpower. The space programme showed that it could equal the technology of the United States – less than 30 years after the start of Stalin's first Five Year Plan the Soviet Union sent a satellite (Sputnik 1) into orbit round the earth. There were many economic problems after the war, but grain production doubled between 1950 and 1980, coal production trebled, ten times as much cement was produced, as well as twelve times as much electricity and fifteen times as much oil.

ment eech), on

1956: Khruschev denounces Stalin at the 20th Party Conference.

Khruschev cancels summit meeting with USA when US spy plane is shot down over Sverdlovsk.

Successful launching of the world's first satellite in 1957 and the first astronaut (Yuri Gagarin) in 1961.

1969: Serious shooting incidents in a border dispute with China.

GOLIA

CHINA   KOREA   JAPAN

1954 onwards: Russia ploughs up the virgin lands of Kazakhstan to grow wheat but fails to produce all the extra grain needed and has to import wheat – some from the USA.

to e.

1960s: Break with China over Russia's policy of peaceful co-existence. China accuses Russia of being 'Revisionist'.

???????????????

1 What have been the main developments in the Soviet Union since the death of Stalin in 1953?

2 What was the significance of (a) Khruschev's denunciation of Stalin in 1956, (b) the development of Russia's space programme, (c) the Russian invasion of Afghanistan in 1979?

The Warsaw Pact Countries

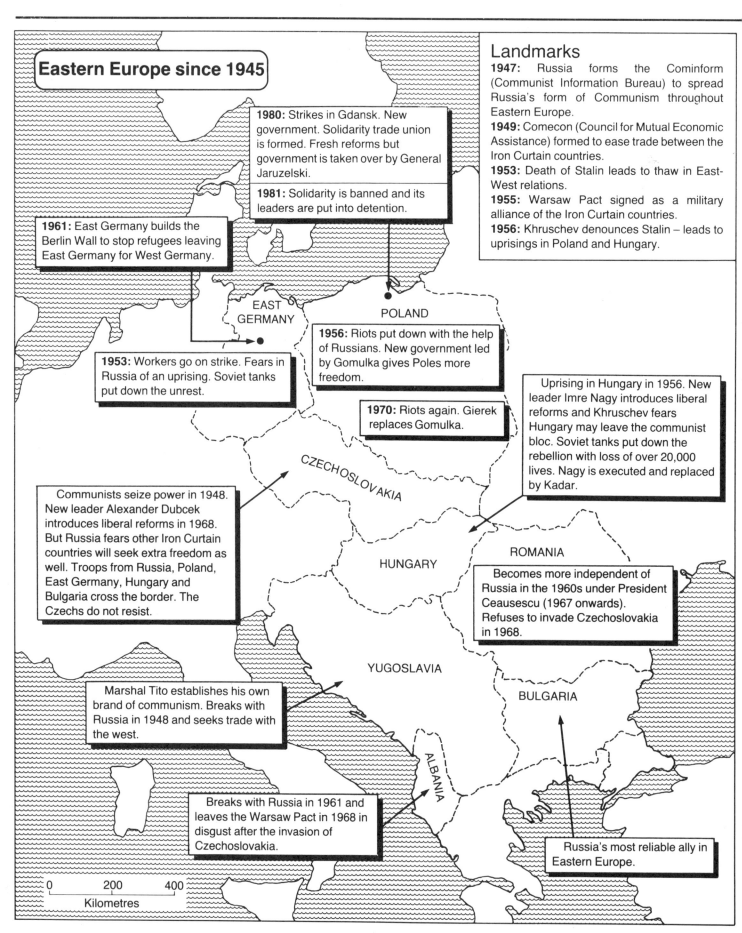

Eastern Europe since 1945

Landmarks

1947: Russia forms the Cominform (Communist Information Bureau) to spread Russia's form of Communism throughout Eastern Europe.

1949: Comecon (Council for Mutual Economic Assistance) formed to ease trade between the Iron Curtain countries.

1953: Death of Stalin leads to thaw in East-West relations.

1955: Warsaw Pact signed as a military alliance of the Iron Curtain countries.

1956: Khruschev denounces Stalin – leads to uprisings in Poland and Hungary.

1980: Strikes in Gdansk. New government. Solidarity trade union is formed. Fresh reforms but government is taken over by General Jaruzelski.

1981: Solidarity is banned and its leaders are put into detention.

1961: East Germany builds the Berlin Wall to stop refugees leaving East Germany for West Germany.

1953: Workers go on strike. Fears in Russia of an uprising. Soviet tanks put down the unrest.

EAST GERMANY

POLAND

1956: Riots put down with the help of Russians. New government led by Gomulka gives Poles more freedom.

1970: Riots again. Gierek replaces Gomulka.

Uprising in Hungary in 1956. New leader Imre Nagy introduces liberal reforms and Khruschev fears Hungary may leave the communist bloc. Soviet tanks put down the rebellion with loss of over 20,000 lives. Nagy is executed and replaced by Kadar.

CZECHOSLOVAKIA

Communists seize power in 1948. New leader Alexander Dubcek introduces liberal reforms in 1968. But Russia fears other Iron Curtain countries will seek extra freedom as well. Troops from Russia, Poland, East Germany, Hungary and Bulgaria cross the border. The Czechs do not resist.

HUNGARY

ROMANIA

Becomes more independent of Russia in the 1960s under President Ceausescu (1967 onwards). Refuses to invade Czechoslovakia in 1968.

YUGOSLAVIA

BULGARIA

Marshal Tito establishes his own brand of communism. Breaks with Russia in 1948 and seeks trade with the west.

ALBANIA

Breaks with Russia in 1961 and leaves the Warsaw Pact in 1968 in disgust after the invasion of Czechoslovakia.

Russia's most reliable ally in Eastern Europe.

0   200   400
Kilometres

Soon after the war, most of the countries 'liberated' by the Red Army turned communist. Opposition was ruthlessly suppressed. Only Yugoslavia (led by Marshal Tito) defied Russia.

Since the death of Stalin in 1953, there have been uprisings and movements towards greater freedom in almost all the countries of Eastern Europe. But the Iron Curtain countries still stick together for mutual protection and trade. When West Germany joined NATO in 1955 the Soviet Union and the countries of Eastern Europe (excluding Yugoslavia) formed the Warsaw Pact. Like NATO this is a military alliance.

Today the Warsaw Pact countries form a unified military bloc, facing NATO. Both sides have nuclear ballistic missiles, military bases and early warning stations in the Arctic north. Both have launched spy satellites to detect any move by the other side. By roughly balancing their forces the two sides have reached a position of nuclear stalemate or 'balance of terror'.

?????????????????????????????

1 How and why have the peoples of Eastern Europe attempted to break free of Russian communism? To what extent have they been successful?
2 What were the principal reasons for the setting up of (a) the Cominform, (b) NATO, (c) the Warsaw Pact?

The Balance of Power in Europe in the 1970s

NATO COUNTRIES		WARSAW PACT COUNTRIES
	AIRCRAFT each symbol = 400 planes	
	TANKS each symbol = 3000 tanks	
	TROOPS each symbol = 100,000 troops	

Countries of Eastern Europe since 1945

COUNTRY		CAPITAL CITY	CITIES over ½ million	IMPORTANT RESOURCES	RELIGION	Member of Comecon	Member of Warsaw Pact	NOTABLE LEADERS SINCE 1945 Government Leaders	Associated with opposition to govt.
GERMAN DEMOCRATIC REPUBLIC	17M	East Berlin	East Berlin Leipzig Dresden	Iron and steel	Protestant	Yes	Yes	Walter Ulbricht Erich Honecker	
POLAND	35M	Warsaw	Warsaw Cracow Wroclaw Poznan Lodz	Coal Iron and steel	Roman Catholic	Yes	Yes	Wladyslaw Gomulka Edward Gierek General Jaruzelski	Cardinal Wyszynski Lech Walesa
CZECHOSLOVAKIA	15M	Prague	Prague	Coal Iron and steel	Roman Catholic	Yes	Yes	Klemens Gottwald Antonin Novotny	Alexander Dubcek
HUNGARY	11M	Budapest	Budapest		Roman Catholic	Yes	Yes	Matyas Rakosi Janos Kadar	Cardinal Mindszenty Imre Nagy
ROMANIA	22M	Bucharest	Bucharest	Oil Natural gas	Orthodox Church	Yes	Yes	Nicolae Ceausescu	
BULGARIA	9M	Sofia	Sofia		Orthodox Church	Yes	Yes	Georgi Dimitrov	
YUGOSLAVIA	22M	Belgrade	Belgrade Zagreb		Orthodox Church and Roman Catholic	No	No	Marshal Tito	
ALBANIA	2.5M	Tirana			Moslem	Left in 1962	Left in 1968	Enver Hoxha	

The United States 1945-1982

The prosperity of the people of the United States grew rapidly after 1945, in contrast to the depression years before the war. Technological achievements backed by an immense wealth of natural resources, easily made the USA the most powerful nation on earth. The nuclear weapons programme, missile development, automation, development of the computer, exploration of space, aircraft design, rapid expansion of consumer products (such as cars, television sets, domestic appliances) helped to make the United States prosperous.

But it was also a period of heightened social tensions – when black Americans fought for justice and equality of opportunity and when students demonstrated against American involvement in the Vietnam War. There were several major political upheavals. After spies had been convicted of passing atom bomb secrets to Russia, Senator Joseph McCarthy began a witchhunt against anyone he suspected of sympathising with the Communist Party (banned in 1954). Many people lost their jobs through his smear campaigns, even though they were innocent.

In 1963 President Kennedy, a young and vigorous leader who seemed to offer hope to the underprivileged of America, was shot dead when visiting Dallas in Texas. In 1974 President Nixon was forced to resign over the Watergate scandal and in 1979 President Carter found he was helpless to intervene when revolutionary guards seized staff of the American Embassy in Teheran.

?????????????????????????????

1 How did the civil rights campaigners draw attention to the grievances of America's black population? How far were they successful in achieving their aims?
2 Which recent American president, in your opinion, has been the most successful both at home and abroad?

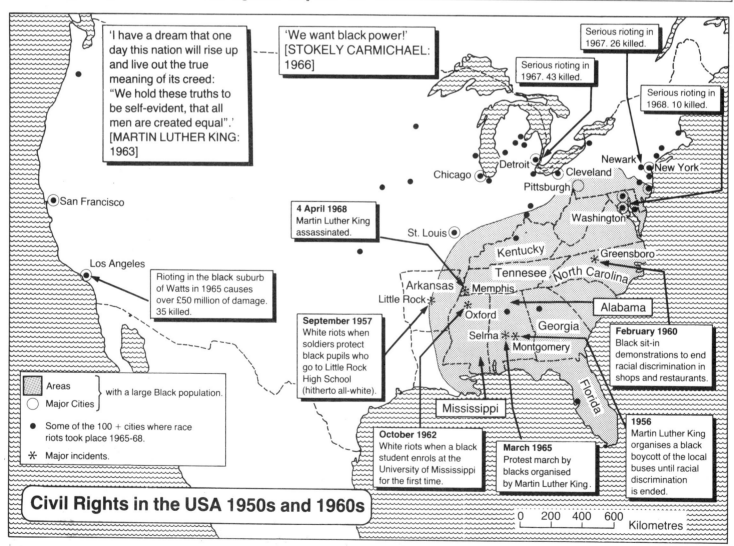

'I have a dream that one day this nation will rise up and live out the true meaning of its creed: "We hold these truths to be self-evident, that all men are created equal".' [MARTIN LUTHER KING: 1963]

'We want black power!' [STOKELY CARMICHAEL: 1966]

Serious rioting in 1967. 26 killed.

Serious rioting in 1967. 43 killed.

Serious rioting in 1968. 10 killed.

4 April 1968 Martin Luther King assassinated.

Rioting in the black suburb of Watts in 1965 causes over £50 million of damage. 35 killed.

September 1957 White riots when soldiers protect black pupils who go to Little Rock High School (hitherto all-white).

February 1960 Black sit-in demonstrations to end racial discrimination in shops and restaurants.

October 1962 White riots when a black student enrols at the University of Mississippi for the first time.

March 1965 Protest march by blacks organised by Martin Luther King.

1956 Martin Luther King organises a black boycott of the local buses until racial discrimination is ended.

Areas } with a large Black population.
◯ Major Cities
● Some of the 100 + cities where race riots took place 1965-68.
✳ Major incidents.

Civil Rights in the USA 1950s and 1960s

0 200 400 600 Kilometres

56

American Presidents since 1945

President	Party	Domestic Policies and Events at Home	Decisions Concerning Foreign Affairs
HARRY S. TRUMAN 1884-1972	Democrat 1945-53	Initiated his **Fair Deal** legislation designed to eliminate poverty, improve public health, establish old age pensions, raise minimum wages, etc. Most of it blocked by Congress (the American Parliament).	Atom bombs on Japan. Marshall Aid to Europe. Truman Doctrine (anti-communist – helped to begin Cold War). Berlin Blockade. Formation of NATO. Korean War. Sacked General MacArthur.
DWIGHT EISENHOWER 1890-1969	Republican 1953-61	As a Republican he tended to back businesss interests rather than those of ordinary people. Upheld Civil Rights when he sent Federal troops to Little Rock to protect black schoolchildren.	Ended the Korean War. His anti-communist Secretary of State, John Foster Dulles, took a hard line on the Cold War. Intervened in a civil war in the Lebanon by sending in US troops. Some peace initiatives but summit meeting with Khruschev (USSR) cancelled when U-2 spy plane shot down.
JOHN F. KENNEDY 1917-1963	Democrat 1961-63	Initiated his **New Frontier** legislation on matters concerning health, renewing cities, civil rights, clearing slums, welfare provision for those in need. Much of it rejected by Congress. Assassinated at Dallas in Texas on 22 November 1963.	Bay of Pigs fiasco. Cuban missile crisis. Backed West Germany over West Berlin and visited the Berlin Wall ('I am a Berliner' he told them). Vietnam War involvement increased. Partial Test Ban Treaty with Russia. Made the decision to go all out to put a man on the moon before Russia did.
LYNDON BAINES JOHNSON 1908-1973	Democrat 1963-69	Wanted a **Great Society.** As a former leader of the US Senate he knew how to get things done and succeeded in persuading Congress to pass many laws – such as improving welfare provision, civil rights, health (Medicare). urban renewal. Senator Robert F. Kennedy, brother of John F. Kennedy and probable Democratic presidential candidate, assassinated in Los Angeles in 1968.	Escalated the Vietnam War by pouring troops into South Vietnam and bombing Hanoi and other cities in North Vietnam. As casualties mounted Demonstrators taunted him with the slogan 'Hey! Hey! LBJ! How many kids did you kill today?'. Intervened in a civil war in the Dominican Republic by sending in US troops to prevent a possible communist takeover.
RICHARD NIXON 1913-	Republican 1969-74	Some social legislation (such as increasing government spending on food stamps for the poor). In July 1969 Armstrong and Aldrin landed on the moon. In June 1972 five men were arrested breaking into Democratic Party offices in the Watergate Building in Washington. It became clear that Republican Party members had sent them and the resulting scandal ended in Nixon's resignation and the imprisonment of several of his closest advisers.	Escalated the Vietnam War by heavy bombing raids on North Vietnam and by sanctioning invasions of Laos and Cambodia; but he did eventually withdraw American forces and negotiate a ceasefire. Together with his Secretary of State, Dr. Kissinger, he worked for detente (easing of tension) between the US and both Russia and China. Visited both countries. Agreed SALT 1 (Strategic Arms Limitation Talks) with Russia.
GERALD FORD 1913-	Republican 1974-1977	Pardoned ex-President Nixon. Growing problem of unemployment and inflation.	Continued the policy of detente with Russia and China. Visited China.
JAMES 'JIMMY' CARTER 1924-	Democrat 1977-81	Social reforms blocked by Congress. Beset with problems arising from the energy crisis, such as inflation and unemployment.	Made human rights an international issue. SALT 2 agreement. Camp David agreement in 1978 between President Sadat of Egypt and Prime Minister Begin of Israel. Ineffective response to the Russian invasion of Afghanistan. Powerless to free American hostages imprisoned in Iran.
RONALD REAGAN 1911-	Republican 1981-	Right-wing Republican. Made huge cuts in government spending on welfare services, Unemployment became a major problem (as in other Western countries). Soup kitchens, dole queues and camps set up by the homeless recalled the Depression years of the 1930s.	Increased spending on defence but plans for further expansion of America's nuclear defences met with growing opposition. Imposed sanctions against Poland when that government clamped down on the Solidarity trade union.

The Cuban Missiles Crisis 1962

In 1823 President Monroe declared that America was outside Europe's sphere of influence (the Monroe Doctrine). Ever since, the Americans have regarded outside interference in American affairs with the gravest suspicion. In 1948 many of the nations of North, Central and South America, jointly formed the OAS (Organization of American States) to settle disputes between member states.

In 1959 the American government looked on with great concern when the Marxist Fidel Castro seized power in Cuba, a Caribbean island less than 200 kilometres from the coast of Florida.

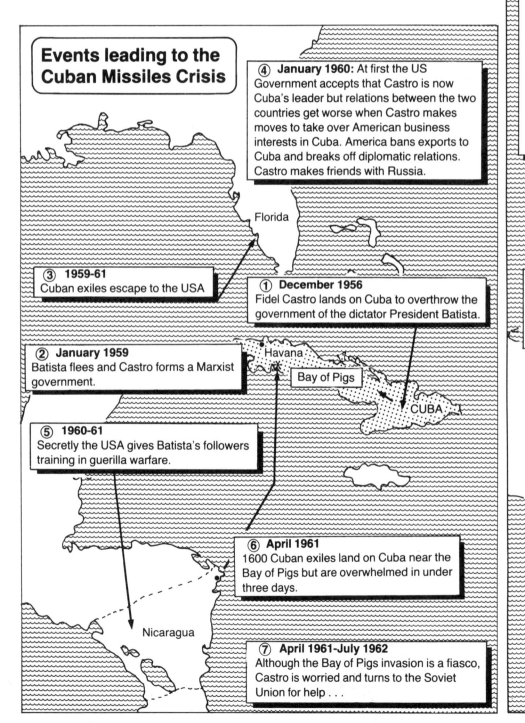

Events leading to the Cuban Missiles Crisis

④ **January 1960:** At first the US Government accepts that Castro is now Cuba's leader but relations between the two countries get worse when Castro makes moves to take over American business interests in Cuba. America bans exports to Cuba and breaks off diplomatic relations. Castro makes friends with Russia.

Florida

③ **1959-61**
Cuban exiles escape to the USA

① **December 1956**
Fidel Castro lands on Cuba to overthrow the government of the dictator President Batista.

② **January 1959**
Batista flees and Castro forms a Marxist government.

Havana

Bay of Pigs

CUBA

⑤ **1960-61**
Secretly the USA gives Batista's followers training in guerilla warfare.

⑥ **April 1961**
1600 Cuban exiles land on Cuba near the Bay of Pigs but are overwhelmed in under three days.

Nicaragua

⑦ **April 1961-July 1962**
Although the Bay of Pigs invasion is a fiasco, Castro is worried and turns to the Soviet Union for help . . .

④ **Monday 22 October**
Kennedy announces a blockade of Cuba. All ships entering the blockade zone will be searched and those carrying weapons will be turned away.

③ **Monday 15 October to Sunday 21 October**
President Kennedy and his advisors discuss what to do. If they bomb the missile sites they may start World War Three. If they do nothing the President will have less than three minutes warning of a Russian missile attack (instead of 15 minutes).

② **Sunday 14 October**
US spy planes take photographs of Russian missile sites being rapidly built in western Cuba.

① **Summer**
Russian ships unload suspicious cargoes at a Cuban port near Havana. Each ship brings with it a large number of Russian engineers.

CENTRAL AMERICA

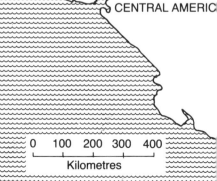

0   100   200   300   400
Kilometres

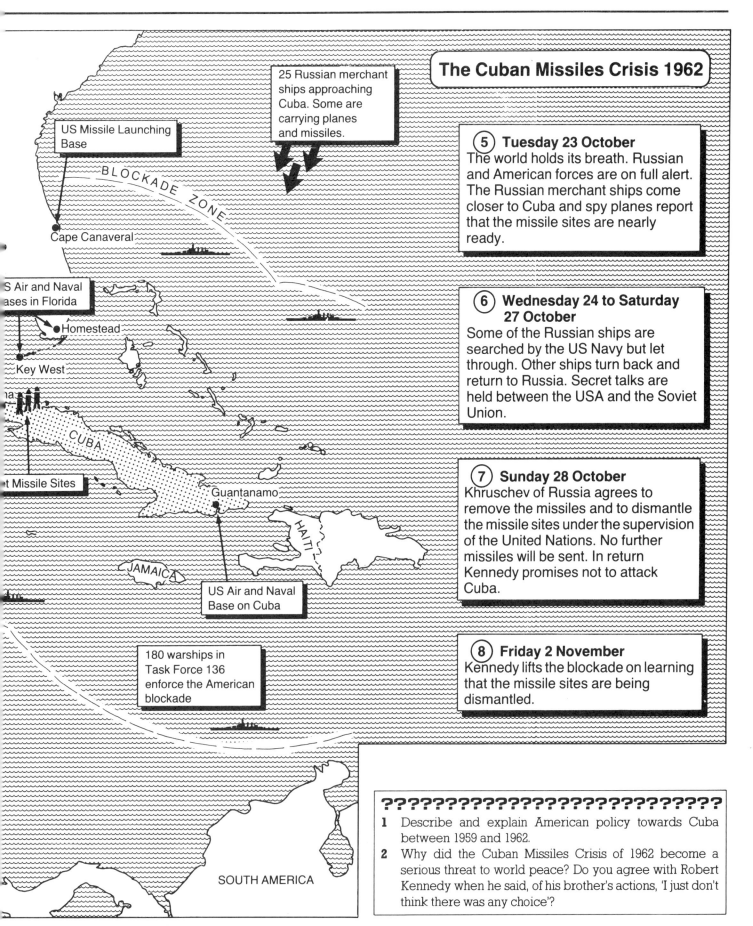

The Cuban Missiles Crisis 1962

25 Russian merchant ships approaching Cuba. Some are carrying planes and missiles.

US Missile Launching Base

BLOCKADE ZONE

Cape Canaveral

US Air and Naval Bases in Florida

Homestead

Key West

CUBA

Missile Sites

Guantanamo

HAITI

JAMAICA

US Air and Naval Base on Cuba

180 warships in Task Force 136 enforce the American blockade

SOUTH AMERICA

(5) Tuesday 23 October
The world holds its breath. Russian and American forces are on full alert. The Russian merchant ships come closer to Cuba and spy planes report that the missile sites are nearly ready.

(6) Wednesday 24 to Saturday 27 October
Some of the Russian ships are searched by the US Navy but let through. Other ships turn back and return to Russia. Secret talks are held between the USA and the Soviet Union.

(7) Sunday 28 October
Khruschev of Russia agrees to remove the missiles and to dismantle the missile sites under the supervision of the United Nations. No further missiles will be sent. In return Kennedy promises not to attack Cuba.

(8) Friday 2 November
Kennedy lifts the blockade on learning that the missile sites are being dismantled.

???????????????????????????

1 Describe and explain American policy towards Cuba between 1959 and 1962.
2 Why did the Cuban Missiles Crisis of 1962 become a serious threat to world peace? Do you agree with Robert Kennedy when he said, of his brother's actions, 'I just don't think there was any choice'?

Vietnam

The map on this page shows the main events which led up to the partition of Vietnam in 1954. Partition was not meant to last. Free elections were to be held in 1956 to reunite the country and Ho Chi Minh, the leader of North Vietnam, believed these would result in a Communist-led Vietnam.

But in 1955 Diem took power in South Vietnam and refused to hold the promised elections. He ruled as a dictator with armed forces trained and paid for by the American government, which feared a Communist takeover in south-east Asia. Ho Chi Minh began to train South Vietnamese communists as guerillas (the Vietcong) to fight Diem's forces. By 1958 the Vietcong were harassing South Vietnamese towns and villages and much of the countryside began to fall into their hands. To counter this the Americans sent soldiers as 'advisers' to train the South Vietnamese armies. In 1963 Diem was murdered, only a few weeks before the assassination of President Kennedy. The new President, Lyndon B. Johnson, was determined not to be 'soft' on communism and within a year America was deeply involved in the war.

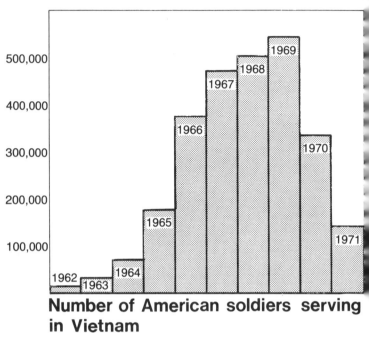

Number of American soldiers serving in Vietnam

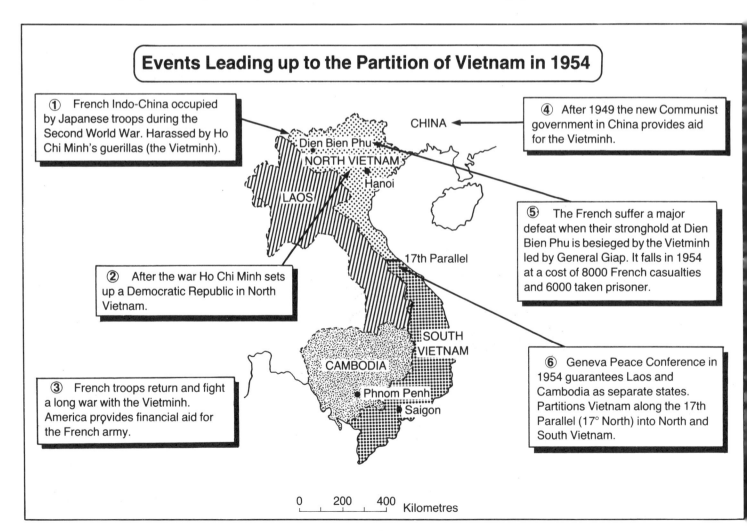

Events Leading up to the Partition of Vietnam in 1954

① French Indo-China occupied by Japanese troops during the Second World War. Harassed by Ho Chi Minh's guerillas (the Vietminh).

④ After 1949 the new Communist government in China provides aid for the Vietminh.

② After the war Ho Chi Minh sets up a Democratic Republic in North Vietnam.

⑤ The French suffer a major defeat when their stronghold at Dien Bien Phu is besieged by the Vietminh led by General Giap. It falls in 1954 at a cost of 8000 French casualties and 6000 taken prisoner.

③ French troops return and fight a long war with the Vietminh. America provides financial aid for the French army.

⑥ Geneva Peace Conference in 1954 guarantees Laos and Cambodia as separate states. Partitions Vietnam along the 17th Parallel (17° North) into North and South Vietnam.

CHINA

Dien Bien Phu
NORTH VIETNAM
Hanoi
LAOS
17th Parallel
SOUTH VIETNAM
CAMBODIA
Phnom Penh
Saigon

0   200   400   Kilometres

What the Vietnam War cost America

★ The lives of nearly 60,000 Americans.

★ About 160,000 wounded service personnel.

★ The loss of prestige and influence abroad – among many Third World nations during the actual fighting *and* among other nations when she withdrew her forces and Vietnam became Communist anyway.

★ In terms of servicemen engaged in fighting it was America's SECOND most important war (after the Second World War).

★ In terms of casualties it was worse than the Korean War and almost as bad as the First World War.

★ It was also America's least successful war, since the only reason why the soldiers fought there was to stop Vietnam becoming Communist – Vietnam became Communist in 1975.

?????????????????????????

1 How and why did American forces become involved in the Vietnam War? Why did they withdraw in 1973? What was the consequence of this action?

2 The Americans were afraid that if South Vietnam became Communist, then Laos, Cambodia, Thailand, Malaysia, Burma, India and other countries would fall like dominoes, one after the other. Has this happened since the fall of Vietnam in 1975?

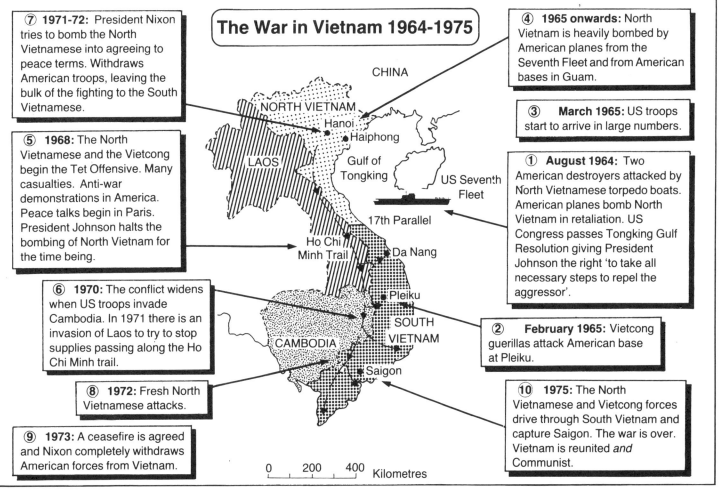

The War in Vietnam 1964-1975

⑦ **1971-72:** President Nixon tries to bomb the North Vietnamese into agreeing to peace terms. Withdraws American troops, leaving the bulk of the fighting to the South Vietnamese.

⑤ **1968:** The North Vietnamese and the Vietcong begin the Tet Offensive. Many casualties. Anti-war demonstrations in America. Peace talks begin in Paris. President Johnson halts the bombing of North Vietnam for the time being.

⑥ **1970:** The conflict widens when US troops invade Cambodia. In 1971 there is an invasion of Laos to try to stop supplies passing along the Ho Chi Minh trail.

⑧ **1972:** Fresh North Vietnamese attacks.

⑨ **1973:** A ceasefire is agreed and Nixon completely withdraws American forces from Vietnam.

④ **1965 onwards:** North Vietnam is heavily bombed by American planes from the Seventh Fleet and from American bases in Guam.

③ **March 1965:** US troops start to arrive in large numbers.

① **August 1964:** Two American destroyers attacked by North Vietnamese torpedo boats. American planes bomb North Vietnam in retaliation. US Congress passes Tongking Gulf Resolution giving President Johnson the right 'to take all necessary steps to repel the aggressor'.

② **February 1965:** Vietcong guerillas attack American base at Pleiku.

⑩ **1975:** The North Vietnamese and Vietcong forces drive through South Vietnam and capture Saigon. The war is over. Vietnam is reunited *and* Communist.

CHINA

NORTH VIETNAM
Hanoi
Haiphong
LAOS
Gulf of Tongking
US Seventh Fleet
17th Parallel
Ho Chi Minh Trail
Da Nang
Pleiku
SOUTH VIETNAM
CAMBODIA
Saigon

0   200   400 Kilometres

Nuclear Weapons and Disarmament

A country wishing to have a strong nuclear deterrent must first get nuclear weapons, and second, work out an effective way of dropping those weapons on the enemy. This is why both the Soviet Union and the United States have built rockets, missiles and space satellites, at the same time developing the atom bomb and the more powerful hydrogen bomb.

Spy planes and satellites in space, armed with cameras, can now photograph the earth's surface in incredible detail. So both the USA and the USSR are believed to know each other's nuclear weapons fairly well. As you can see from the graph both countries were roughly able to match each other's nuclear strike power in 1980.

????????????????????????????

Examine the contribution of any three of the following towards a reduction in the likelihood of nuclear war since 1945: (a) the after effects of Hiroshima and Nagasaki, (b) the Cuban Missiles Crisis 1962, (c) the Hotline between Russia and the USA 1963, (d) the Test Ban Treaty 1963, (e) the Non-Proliferation Treaty 1968, (f) the SALT treaties 1972-78, (g) protest movements such as the Campaign for Nuclear Disarmament.

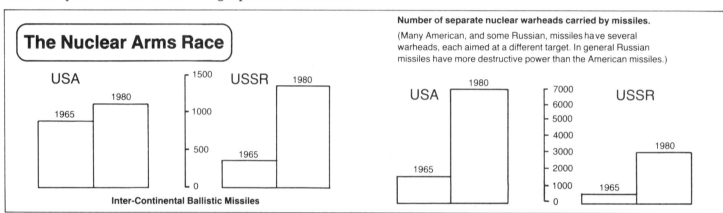

The Nuclear Arms Race

USA — 1965, 1980
USSR — 1965, 1980
Inter-Continental Ballistic Missiles

Number of separate nuclear warheads carried by missiles.

(Many American, and some Russian, missiles have several warheads, each aimed at a different target. In general Russian missiles have more destructive power than the American missiles.)

USA — 1965, 1980
USSR — 1965, 1980

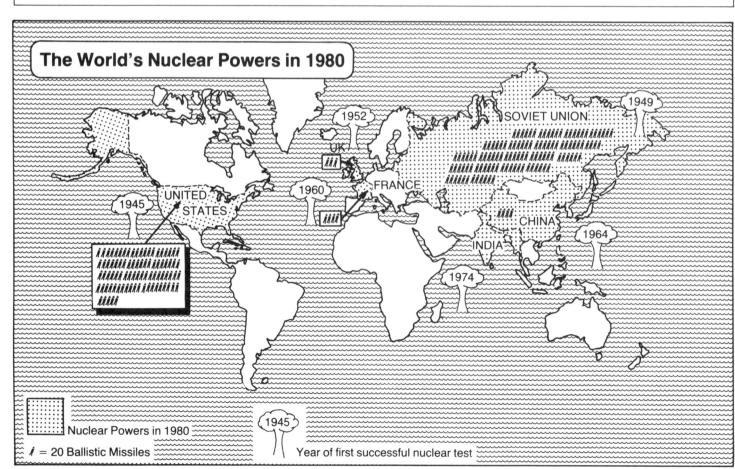

The World's Nuclear Powers in 1980

1952 — UK
1949 — SOVIET UNION
1960 — FRANCE
1945 — UNITED STATES
CHINA — 1964
INDIA — 1974

Nuclear Powers in 1980
= 20 Ballistic Missiles
1945 — Year of first successful nuclear test

Time Line

1943 Top scientists work in the USA on the Manhattan Project to develop an atom bomb. Britain and America fear that German scientists may make one first.

1944 Germany launches the V-1 flying bomb and the V-2 rocket – the world's first effective missile weapons.

1945 **17 July:** World's first atom bomb successfully tested in New Mexico (USA).

6-9 August: Atom bombs dropped with horrific consequences on Hiroshima and Nagasaki (an estimated 150,000 eventually die) but the war against Japan ends.

1949 Soviet atom bomb.

1952 British atom bomb. American hydrogen bomb.

1953 Soviet hydrogen bomb.

1957 British hydrogen bomb. Soviet Union launches Sputnik 1 – the world's first space satellite. The Space Race begins between Russia and America to build bigger and better rockets.

1960 French atom bomb.

1963 Test Ban Treaty bans nuclear tests in space, in the sea or in the air. Only underground tests are permitted. But France and China do not sign the Treaty. 'Hotline' telephone link set up between the White House and the Kremlin – to enable the superpowers to get in touch immediately in an emergency.

1964 Chinese atom bomb.

1968 French and Chinese hydrogen bombs. USSR, USA and UK sign the Non-Proliferation Treaty to stop the spread of nuclear weapons to other countries.

1972 SALT 1 talks. Strategic Arms Limitation Treaty signed by USA and USSR limiting the number of nuclear ballistic missiles held by each side.

1974 Indian atom bomb.

1978 SALT 2 agreement; but later suspended by America after the Russian invasion of Afghanistan.

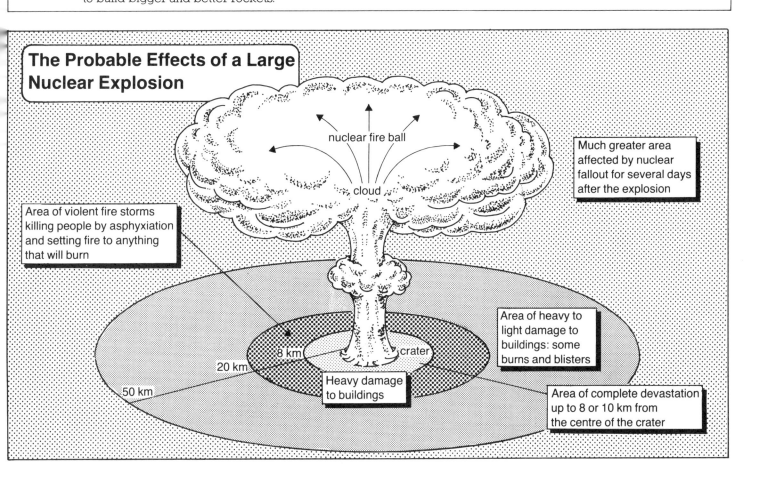

The Probable Effects of a Large Nuclear Explosion

nuclear fire ball

cloud

Much greater area affected by nuclear fallout for several days after the explosion

Area of violent fire storms killing people by asphyxiation and setting fire to anything that will burn

8 km

20 km

50 km

crater

Heavy damage to buildings

Area of heavy to light damage to buildings: some burns and blisters

Area of complete devastation up to 8 or 10 km from the centre of the crater

France and Germany since 1945

Before 1945 France and Germany were rivals and enemies. They fought in 1870, 1914 and 1939. But since 1945, these two powerful and prosperous countries have combined together to work towards European unity. As France gave up her overseas possessions (such as French Indo-China, Algeria and French Equatorial Africa) she grew closer to the other countries of Europe through the development of the European Community. At the same time a technological and industrial revolution took place in France. In the period 1945-75 she overtook the United Kingdom in industrial output in several important spheres – for instance, producing more iron and steel and many more motor vehicles. Germany too prospered. Millions of American dollars helped to restore the coalfields of the Ruhr and other German industrial areas. By 1960 she was the richest country in Europe once more – a feat so remarkable the Germans called it the *Wirtschaftswunder* or 'economic miracle'.

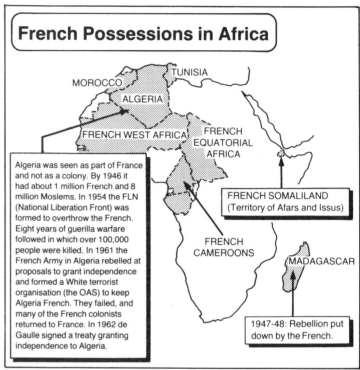

French Possessions in Africa

Algeria was seen as part of France and not as a colony. By 1946 it had about 1 million French and 8 million Moslems. In 1954 the FLN (National Liberation Front) was formed to overthrow the French. Eight years of guerilla warfare followed in which over 100,000 people were killed. In 1961 the French Army in Algeria rebelled at proposals to grant independence and formed a White terrorist organisation (the OAS) to keep Algeria French. They failed, and many of the French colonists returned to France. In 1962 de Gaulle signed a treaty granting independence to Algeria.

1947-48: Rebellion put down by the French.

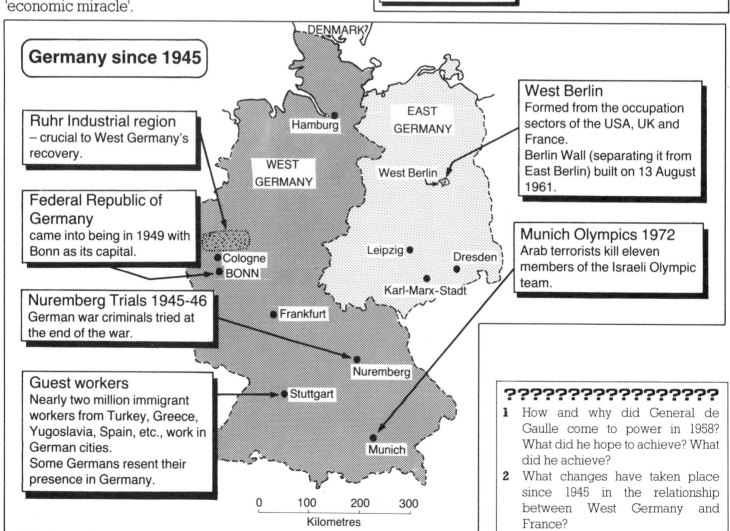

Germany since 1945

Ruhr Industrial region
– crucial to West Germany's recovery.

Federal Republic of Germany
came into being in 1949 with Bonn as its capital.

Nuremberg Trials 1945-46
German war criminals tried at the end of the war.

Guest workers
Nearly two million immigrant workers from Turkey, Greece, Yugoslavia, Spain, etc., work in German cities.
Some Germans resent their presence in Germany.

West Berlin
Formed from the occupation sectors of the USA, UK and France.
Berlin Wall (separating it from East Berlin) built on 13 August 1961.

Munich Olympics 1972
Arab terrorists kill eleven members of the Israeli Olympic team.

0   100   200   300
Kilometres

???????????????????

1 How and why did General de Gaulle come to power in 1958? What did he hope to achieve? What did he achieve?

2 What changes have taken place since 1945 in the relationship between West Germany and France?

Time Chart

DATE	GERMANY	FRANCE	DATE
1945	Occupied by the four allies. Denazification (former Nazi Party members investigated). Nuremberg Trials of leading Nazi war criminals.	Occupies French zone in Germany. Provisional government led by General de Gaulle.	**1945**
1946	American aid helps to put both Germany and France back on their feet after the devastation caused by the war.	De Gaulle resigns. Fourth Republic formed. In the next twelve years France has 25 different governments. War in Indo-China begins.	**1946**
1947	The three western zones merge into one.	The Monnet Plan helps French industry and agriculture to modernise.	**1947**
1948	Berlin Blockade begins. The Allies airlift supplies.		
1949	Berlin Blockade ends. Federal Republic of Germany is founded. First elections to a German parliament (the Bundestag) since 1933. Konrad Adenauer becomes Chancellor.	Robert Schuman and Jean· Monnet propose an idea which could help to unify Europe. The Schuman Plan, as it is called, leads to the formation of the European Coal and Steel Community.	**1950**
1951	GERMANY AND FRANCE JOIN THE EUROPEAN COAL AND STEEL COMMUNITY. AGREEMENT SIGNED AT THE TREATY OF PARIS.		**1951**
1952	West Germany virtually free from Allied interference but the troops stay.		
1950s	West Germany makes a remarkable economic recovery. Industry thrives and production rapidly increases. Many new factories and works are built with the profits.	French industry continues to thrive and many new factories and works are built and old ones modernised.	**1950s**
		French defeat at Dien Bien Phu. French pull out of Indo-China	**1954**
1955	West Germany joins NATO.		
1957	GERMANY AND FRANCE HELP TO FORM THE EUROPEAN ECONOMIC COMMUNITY. AGREEMENT SIGNED AT THE TREATY OF ROME.		
1958	Fresh Berlin crisis. Russia demands withdrawal of Allied troops but the demand is resisted and settled peacefully.	End of Fourth Republic. Crisis in Algeria. De Gaulle is recalled to power and the Fifth Republic is formed. Soon most of the French African possessions become independent.	**1958**
1960	Germany is now the richest and most prosperous country in Europe.	France successfully explodes an atom bomb – the fourth country to do so. De Gaulle wants France to be great again.	**1960**
1961	Berlin Wall erected.	OAS (French army's terrorist organisation in Algeria) revolts against de Gaulle but rebellion is put down.	**1961**
		De Gaulle grants independence to Algeria.	**1962**
1963	President Kennedy visits West Berlin.	De Gaulle vetoes Britain's application to join the EEC.	**1963**
	GERMANY AND FRANCE SIGN A TREATY OF FRIENDSHIP		
1965	The level of unemployment is so low that immigrant workers from Spain, Greece, Italy, Turkey, Yugoslavia flock to Germany in search of jobs.	France withdraws temporarily from participation in Common Market affairs.	**1965**
		France leaves NATO. Unemployment has begun to be a serious problem.	**1966**
1968	Student unrest.	Student unrest in Paris. Street fighting and rioting. Workers demand improved working conditions. Troops are brought in.	**1968**
1969	Willy Brandt (former Mayor of West Berlin) becomes Chancellor. His main policy in foreign affairs is *Ostpolitik* – seeking agreements and friendships with the Eastern bloc.	De Gaulle manages to quell the riots but loses popularity as a result. When a majority of the French people vote NO in a referendum he resigns. Pompidou becomes President.	**1969**
1970	Treaties with Poland and Soviet Union agreeing borders and pledging non-aggression.	De Gaulle dies.	**1970**
1971	Berlin Agreement signed, allowing more access from West to East Berlin.	France no longer objects to British membership of the EEC.	**1971**
1972	Arrest of the Baader-Meinhof Gang – a group of young urban terrorists who commit crimes for political reasons.		
1973	Treaty with East Germany.		
1974	Helmut Schmidt becomes Chancellor.	Giscard d'Estaing becomes President.	**1974**
1975	West Germany begins to feel the effects of the world recession following the sharp rise in oil prices. Unemployment grows. The numbers of immigrant workers coming into Germany are reduced. Schmidt manages to keep wage increases down and prices increase by only 40% in the seven years from 1972 to 1979.	The Lome Convention links former French possessions to the Common Market. France too is feeling the effects of the world recession. D'Estaing is less successful than Schmidt in keeping inflation down and prices rise by about 100% between 1972 and 1979 (although they go up by over 150% in the UK).	**1975**
		François Mitterand, a Socialist, becomes President.	**1981**

The Common Market

After the war there were several moves towards a more united Europe. In 1948 there was a military treaty (*Brussels*) between Britain, France, Holland and Belgium; an economic organisation (OEEC – *Organisation for European Economic Co-operation*) to allocate Marshall Aid; and a meeting place or forum for discussion about European affairs (the *Council of Europe*). Later there were other military agreements (the founding of *NATO* in 1949), and other economic organisations (*EFTA* – the European Free Trade Area which was established in 1959). But it was the Common Market (later the European Community) which pointed the way forward to a united Europe.

Time Line

1951	Treaty of Paris. The six (Germany, France, Italy, Belgium, Luxembourg and Netherlands) agree to join together to found the European Coal and Steel Community (ECSC) – to plan the joint production of coal and steel in the six member states. This works so well it is followed by:
1957	Treaty of Rome. The Six now agree to establish the European Economic Community (EEC) and Euratom (European Atomic Energy Community). They aim to do away with tariffs (import duties) on goods traded from one Common Market country to another.
1959	A rival organisation, EFTA (European Free Trade Association), is formed to assist trade between Austria, Denmark, Norway, Portugal, Sweden, Switzerland and the United Kingdom.
1962	EEC members agree to have a common agricultural policy (CAP) to keep up food prices for wheat, butter and other produce, to help the farmers of the Community.
1963	President de Gaulle vetoes Britain's application to join the Common Market. Talks with Ireland, Denmark and Norway also break down.
1965	France withdraws temporarily from Common Market affairs after a dispute with the other five member states.
1967	The United Kingdom and the other three countries reapply to join the EEC but Britain's application is again vetoed by de Gaulle. However, discussions in 1970 (when de Gaulle has resigned the Presidency of France) go well.
1973	United Kingdom, Denmark and Ireland join the European Community. Norway votes against joining.
1975	Britain's Labour Party holds a National Referendum and 2 people in every 3 vote to stay in the European Community.
1979	Direct elections to the European Parliament (i.e., people vote in all nine countries for an MP to represent them in Europe).
1981	Greece becomes the tenth member of the European Community.

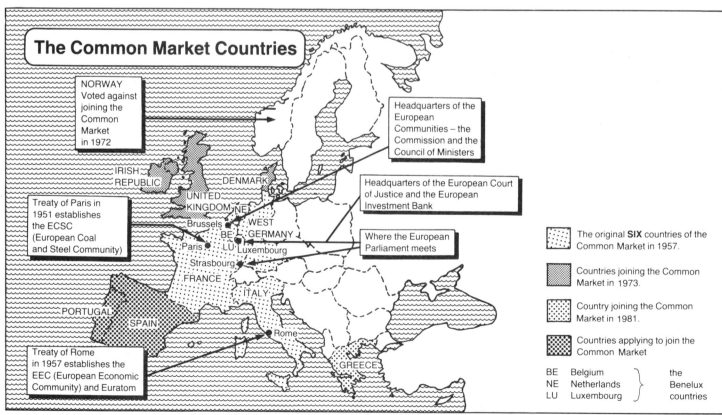

The Common Market Countries

NORWAY Voted against joining the Common Market in 1972

Headquarters of the European Communities – the Commission and the Council of Ministers

Headquarters of the European Court of Justice and the European Investment Bank

Where the European Parliament meets

Treaty of Paris in 1951 establishes the ECSC (European Coal and Steel Community)

Treaty of Rome in 1957 establishes the EEC (European Economic Community) and Euratom

IRISH REPUBLIC · DENMARK · UNITED KINGDOM · NE · Brussels · WEST GERMANY · BE · LU · Paris · Luxembourg · Strasbourg · FRANCE · ITALY · PORTUGAL · SPAIN · Rome · GREECE

The original **SIX** countries of the Common Market in 1957.

Countries joining the Common Market in 1973.

Country joining the Common Market in 1981.

Countries applying to join the Common Market

BE Belgium
NE Netherlands
LU Luxembourg
} the Benelux countries

Some of the Achievements of the European Community

1 Former enemies (Germany and Italy against France and the UK) are now friends and members of the same 'community'.

2 European Parliament elected directly by voters in the member countries.

3 Abolition of customs duties on trade between member countries.

4 No restriction on movement of workers from one member country to another.

5 Many regulations and standards are now common to all the member countries. This is one reason why the British Government introduced Value Added Tax (VAT), and metric measurements and metric currency instead of the old pounds, shillings and pence.

6 Encouragement to European farmers to be more efficient by guaranteeing prices (although this has meant higher prices in the supermarkets and helped to create huge surpluses of foods such as butter, wine and barley).

7 Grants to encourage industrialists to build factories in areas with above-average poverty and high levels of unemployment.

8 Has created an influential voice in world affairs – representing 250 million people. Common Market ministers have made important statements on the Middle East and joined together to block the export of weapons to Argentina during the Falklands Conflict between the UK and Argentina in 1982.

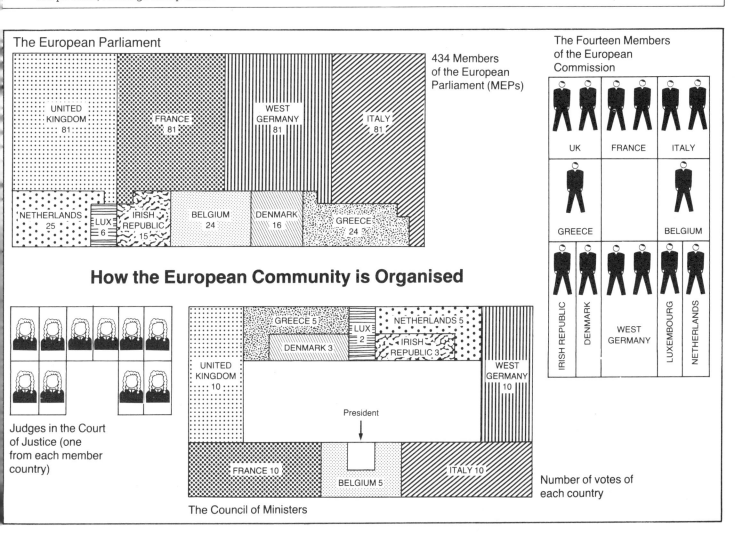

The European Parliament

434 Members of the European Parliament (MEPs)

UNITED KINGDOM 81 · FRANCE 81 · WEST GERMANY 81 · ITALY 81

NETHERLANDS 25 · LUX 6 · IRISH REPUBLIC 15 · BELGIUM 24 · DENMARK 16 · GREECE 24

The Fourteen Members of the European Commission

UK · FRANCE · ITALY · GREECE · BELGIUM · IRISH REPUBLIC · DENMARK · WEST GERMANY · LUXEMBOURG · NETHERLANDS

How the European Community is Organised

Judges in the Court of Justice (one from each member country)

The Council of Ministers

GREECE 5 · LUX 2 · NETHERLANDS 5 · DENMARK 3 · IRISH REPUBLIC 3 · UNITED KINGDOM 10 · WEST GERMANY 10 · President · FRANCE 10 · BELGIUM 5 · ITALY 10

Number of votes of each country

??

1 Why was British entry to the EEC opposed by France? What were the main advantages and disadvantages to Britain of membership of the Community in 1973?

2 Critics of the European Community would disagree that the eight points listed in the table are 'achievements'. Find arguments for and against each statement and say how far you agree with either point of view.

Decolonisation

In 1920 there were territories of the British Empire in almost every corner of the globe, covering 25% of the earth's land surface. By 1980 only the smallest or most vulnerable of these territories had still to gain independence.

The first countries to become fully independent were the white dominions of Canada, Australia, New Zealand, South Africa and Newfoundland. In 1914 they had their own parliaments and laws but Britain still controlled their relations with foreign countries. So when Britain went to war in Europe in 1914, the Dominions also had to go to war, even though the fighting took place thousands of kilometres from their boundaries. Many Empire servicemen lost their lives in the war and the post-war governments were no longer prepared to be drawn into another war without prior consultation. In 1926 Britain and the Dominions agreed that they were all (a) self-governing, (b) equal in status, (c) in no way subordinate to each other, (d) united in a common allegiance to the Crown, (e) free members of the British Commonwealth of Nations. This was put into law by the Statute of Westminster in 1931.

In the 1930s the people of India also sought independence and gained this after demonstrations and rioting in 1947 (see page 46). Black Nationalist leaders in Africa could see no reason why their countries too should not be granted independence. Many had fought in the Second World War to liberate countries, like Belgium and the Netherlands, which had been conquered and enslaved by Nazi Germany. Many had been

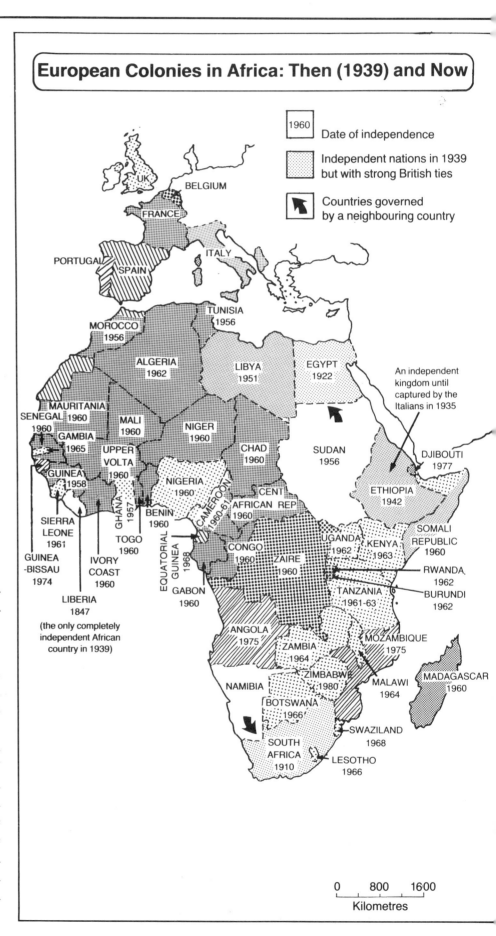

European Colonies in Africa: Then (1939) and Now

Conflict in Africa (since 1945)

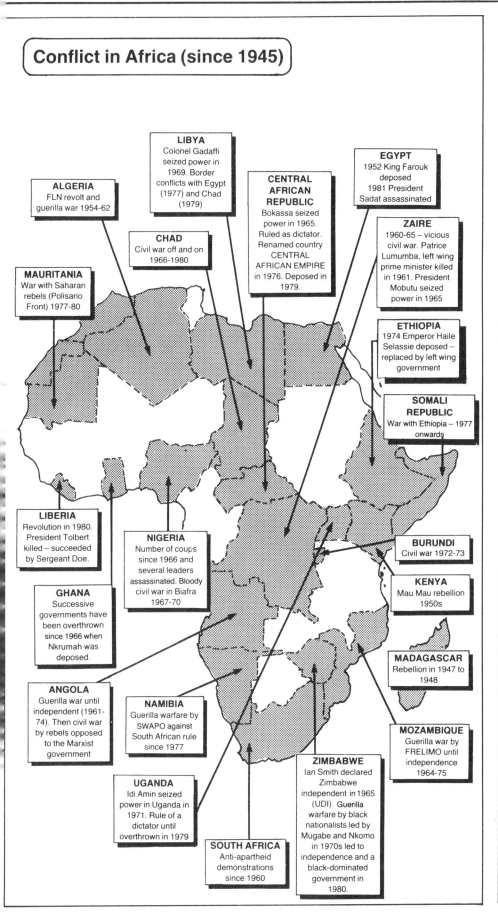

ALGERIA
FLN revolt and guerilla war 1954-62

LIBYA
Colonel Gadaffi seized power in 1969. Border conflicts with Egypt (1977) and Chad (1979)

EGYPT
1952 King Farouk deposed
1981 President Sadat assassinated

CENTRAL AFRICAN REPUBLIC
Bokassa seized power in 1965. Ruled as dictator. Renamed country CENTRAL AFRICAN EMPIRE in 1976. Deposed in 1979.

CHAD
Civil war off and on 1966-1980

ZAIRE
1960-65 – vicious civil war. Patrice Lumumba, left wing prime minister killed in 1961. President Mobutu seized power in 1965

MAURITANIA
War with Saharan rebels (Polisario Front) 1977-80

ETHIOPIA
1974 Emperor Haile Selassie deposed – replaced by left wing government

SOMALI REPUBLIC
War with Ethiopia – 1977 onwards

LIBERIA
Revolution in 1980. President Tolbert killed – succeeded by Sergeant Doe.

NIGERIA
Number of coups since 1966 and several leaders assassinated. Bloody civil war in Biafra 1967-70

BURUNDI
Civil war 1972-73

KENYA
Mau Mau rebellion 1950s

GHANA
Successive governments have been overthrown since 1966 when Nkrumah was deposed.

MADAGASCAR
Rebellion in 1947 to 1948

ANGOLA
Guerilla war until independent (1961-74). Then civil war by rebels opposed to the Marxist government

NAMIBIA
Guerilla warfare by SWAPO against South African rule since 1977

MOZAMBIQUE
Guerilla war by FRELIMO until independence 1964-75

UGANDA
Idi Amin seized power in Uganda in 1971. Rule of a dictator until overthrown in 1979

SOUTH AFRICA
Anti-apartheid demonstrations since 1960

ZIMBABWE
Ian Smith declared Zimbabwe independent in 1965 (UDI). Guerilla warfare by black nationalists led by Mugabe and Nkomo in 1970s led to independence and a black-dominated government in 1980.

educated in Europe or North America and been taught the virtues of democracy and freedom. This experience contrasted with life in their own countries where government was completely in the hands of the colonial powers, such as France, Belgium, Portugal or the United Kingdom. The collapse of the French empire in Indo-China (1954), granting of independence to India, Pakistan, Burma and Sri Lanka by Britain (1947-48) and to Indonesia by the Netherlands (1949) stimulated demands for self-government. Some countries achieved this without a struggle; in other countries such as Kenya (British), Mozambique (Portuguese) and Algeria (French), freedom came only after a long period of guerilla warfare against the colonial governments.

?????????????????

1 In 1960 the British Prime Minister, Harold Macmillan, told South African members of parliament 'The wind of change is blowing through this continent'. What did he mean by this phrase? Look at the two maps and describe the events which had occurred by then to show that Africa was changing fast. Which countries gained their independence within five years of his speech?

2 Compare the two maps. Which African colonies gained their independence (a) after a long guerilla war (b) without a major rebellion? Which African countries have suffered civil wars in the period since independence?

The Third World: Rich and Poor

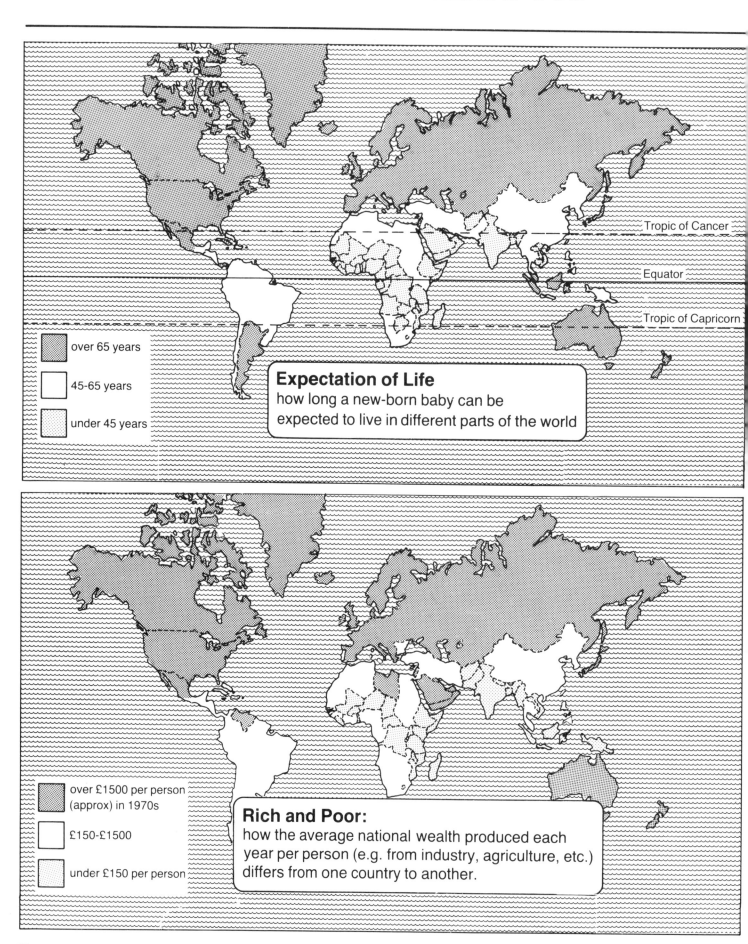

Tropic of Cancer

Equator

Tropic of Capricorn

over 65 years

45-65 years

under 45 years

Expectation of Life
how long a new-born baby can be
expected to live in different parts of the world

over £1500 per person
(approx) in 1970s

£150-£1500

under £150 per person

Rich and Poor:
how the average national wealth produced each
year per person (e.g. from industry, agriculture, etc.)
differs from one country to another.

Most of the more advanced, richer countries of the world are allies of the two great superpowers – either of the United States (the West) or of the Soviet Union (the Iron Curtain countries). Most of the other nations in the world have taken a neutral position. Sometimes they agree with the West (such as the general condemnation of the Russian invasion of Afghanistan in 1979) and sometimes with the Iron Curtain countries (such as the worldwide opposition to American involvement in Vietnam). Sometimes, through the leadership of people like Mrs Gandhi of India, or President Tito of Yugoslavia, they have put a third alternative viewpoint. It is for this reason that these nations have come to be known as the Third World – non-communist, non-Western countries.

Because many of these Third World countries are less advanced than the two superpowers and their allies, they are often described as being *underdeveloped* nations or *developing countries*. Mineral, industrial and agricultural resources have still to be developed on modern lines. Almost all the countries of the developing world are situated in Africa, Asia and South and Central America. Many are former colonies of the European powers.

Their total production of wealth – from agriculture and industry – is usually (but not always) much lower than that of the advanced countries. On average people in the developing countries do not live as long as the peoples of the developed world mainly because of malnutrition and poor medical care. Their homes are much less likely to have a piped water supply (99 in every 100 English homes; 3 in every 100 in Indonesia), a toilet, bathroom or electricity supply (less than 1 home in every 10 in Sri Lanka).

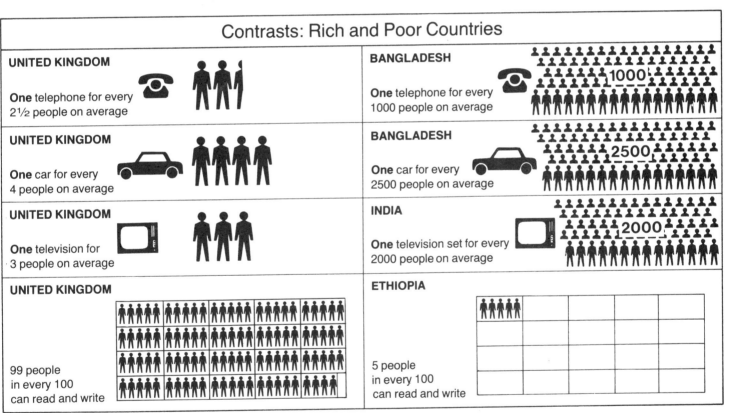

Contrasts: Rich and Poor Countries

UNITED KINGDOM
One telephone for every 2½ people on average

BANGLADESH
One telephone for every 1000 people on average

UNITED KINGDOM
One car for every 4 people on average

BANGLADESH
One car for every 2500 people on average

UNITED KINGDOM
One television for 3 people on average

INDIA
One television set for every 2000 people on average

UNITED KINGDOM
99 people in every 100 can read and write

ETHIOPIA
5 people in every 100 can read and write

???

1 Compare the two world maps. In what ways are they different? Which of the richer countries has a much lower expectation of life for its people than that of other wealthy countries? How do you account for this? Between which two lines of latitude are most of the poor countries situated?

2 Several ways of measuring differences between developing and advanced countries are shown on these maps and diagrams and in the statistics quoted in the text. If you were the leader of a developing country which would you pay most attention to? Why?

Apartheid in South Africa

Apartheid means 'segregation' in Afrikaans, the official language of South Africa. It means not allowing black people to mix with white people – literally keeping them apart. Laws have been passed forbidding mixed marriages; children are educated in separate schools; patients are treated in different hospitals. Other laws limit the freedom of black and coloured people to get jobs, find homes and move from place to place. They have to carry a passbook everywhere and produce it when asked. White people do not have to carry a passbook. When black people protested peacefully against this law in 1960 many were killed by police at a town called Sharpeville.

Only white people can become members of the South African parliament and only white people can vote – yet there are five times as many black, Asian and coloured people in South Africa. Since the 1950s the countries of Africa have gained their independence. But in South Africa the black majority has only been offered independence within the black homelands, or *bantustans*. These are scattered areas of land inside South Africa. Even though there are so many more blacks, Asians and coloureds than whites there are still eight square kilometres in white South Africa, for every square kilometre of land in the black homelands.

Where South Africa's Peoples live

	WHITES (People of English and Dutch descent – the Afrikaaners)	COLOUREDS (People of mixed race)	ASIANS (People of Indian descent in the main)	BLACK AFRICANS (the Bantu)
In FIVE leading cities: Johannesburg, Capetown, Durban, Pretoria and Port Elizabeth	♟♟♟♟♟♟	♟♟♟♟	♟♟	♟♟♟♟♟♟♟
In the rest of South Africa (including farms, villages and the smaller towns and cities)	♟♟♟♟♟♟♟♟	♟♟♟♟♟	♟	♟♟♟♟♟♟♟♟♟ ♟♟♟♟♟♟♟♟♟ ♟♟♟♟♟♟♟♟♟ ♟♟♟♟♟♟♟♟♟ ♟♟♟♟♟♟♟♟♟ ♟♟♟♟♟

Each figure = 250,000 people

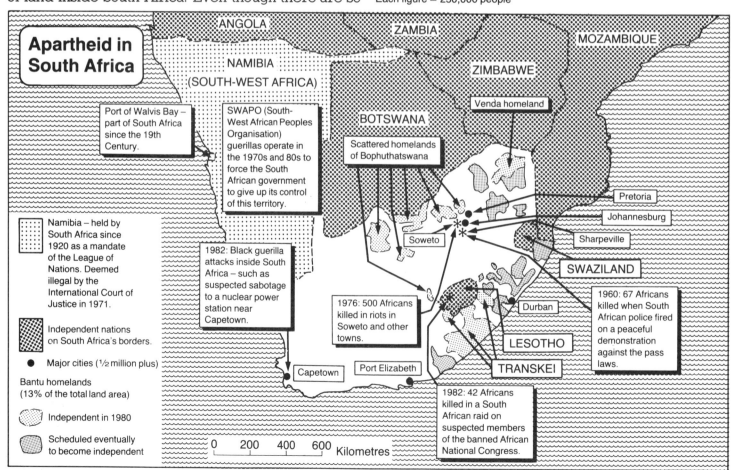

Apartheid in South Africa

Port of Walvis Bay – part of South Africa since the 19th Century.

SWAPO (South-West African Peoples Organisation) guerillas operate in the 1970s and 80s to force the South African government to give up its control of this territory.

Venda homeland

BOTSWANA

Scattered homelands of Bophuthatswana

Pretoria

Johannesburg

Sharpeville

Soweto

SWAZILAND

1960: 67 Africans killed when South African police fired on a peaceful demonstration against the pass laws.

Namibia – held by South Africa since 1920 as a mandate of the League of Nations. Deemed illegal by the International Court of Justice in 1971.

1982: Black guerilla attacks inside South Africa – such as suspected sabotage to a nuclear power station near Capetown.

1976: 500 Africans killed in riots in Soweto and other towns.

Durban

Independent nations on South Africa's borders.

● Major cities (½ million plus)

Bantu homelands (13% of the total land area)

Independent in 1980

Scheduled eventually to become independent

Capetown

Port Elizabeth

LESOTHO

TRANSKEI

1982: 42 Africans killed in a South African raid on suspected members of the banned African National Congress.

0   200   400   600   Kilometres

ANGOLA

ZAMBIA

MOZAMBIQUE

NAMIBIA (SOUTH-WEST AFRICA)

ZIMBABWE

Time Line

1948 The Nationalist Party (led by Afrikaaners descended from Dutch settlers) is elected on a policy of apartheid. Malan is the first Nationalist Party prime minister, followed by Strijdom, Verwoerd, Vorster and Botha.

1949 Mixed marriages are forbidden by law.

1952 Chief Luthuli and Nelson Mandela of the African National Congress (ANC) organise peaceful protests against the new apartheid laws.

1959 The government starts its policy of independent black homelands (bantustans).

1960 Harold Macmillan (Britain's prime minister) tells the South African parliament that 'the wind of change' is blowing through Africa and that people will have to alter their policies. Massacre at Sharpeville. The government bans the ANC. Chief Luthuli gets the Nobel Peace Prize.

1961 South Africa becomes a republic and leaves the Commonwealth.

1963 Nelson Mandela and other leaders of the ANC are sentenced to life imprisonment.

1976 The Transkei becomes the first independent homeland but this is not accepted by foreign countries.

The government tries to make Afrikaans the official language in black schools. This is bitterly resented by the black community and leads to unrest, and then riots, in which about 500 people are killed.

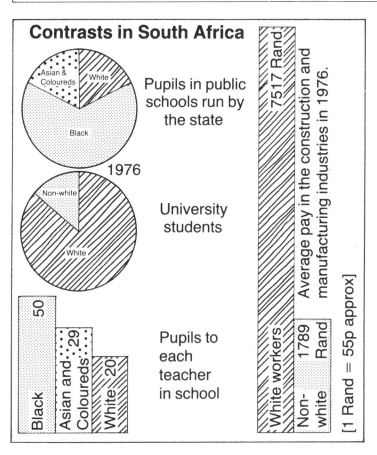

Contrasts in South Africa

Pupils in public schools run by the state — 1976
(Asian & Coloureds, White, Black)

University students
(Non-white, White)

Pupils to each teacher in school:
Black 50
Asian and Coloureds 29
White 20

Average pay in the construction and manufacturing industries in 1976.
White workers 7517 Rand
Non-white 1789 Rand
[1 Rand = 55p approx]

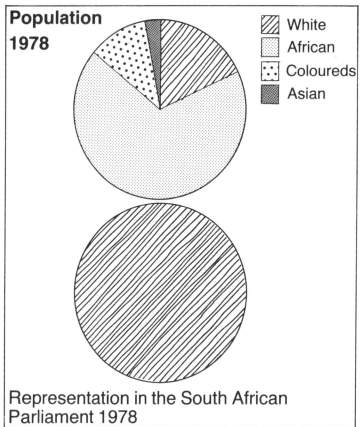

Population 1978

Legend:
- White
- African
- Coloureds
- Asian

Representation in the South African Parliament 1978

??

1 Describe in some detail what is meant by apartheid. How and why did it develop in South Africa in the years following 1948?

2 What are the black homelands? Why has the outside world ignored the existence of these bantustans?

The Palestine Problem to 1967

The Jewish people originally lived in Palestine well over 2000 years ago; but even then were often persecuted and driven from their homeland. By the late nineteenth century most of the world's Jews lived in eastern Europe in lands ruled by Russia. Violent campaigns of persecution (called *pogroms*) in the 1880s forced many to emigrate and over three million Jews settled in the United States.

Some Jews, the Zionists, wanted to set up an independent Jewish state, where Jews could live without fear of anti-Semitism. Before 1914 many Jews emigrated to Palestine, then part of the Ottoman (Turkish) Empire. They set up farms, called *Kibbutzim*, where all the workers lived in a commune, sharing their property and bringing up their children together.

Time Line

1917 A. J. Balfour, the British Foreign Secretary, says in a letter that the British government favours 'the establishment of a national home for the Jewish people'.

1920 Palestine is ruled by the British as a mandate of the League of Nations. Jewish immigration is encouraged.

1929 Arabs living in Palestine resent Jewish settlement. They attack the Jews. Many Jews killed.

1933 Nazis rise to power in Germany. Many more European Jews come to Palestine.

1936 More Arab violence against Jewish settlers and the British. The Arabs fear they may soon be outnumbered.

1939 Britain puts off plans to partition (divide) Palestine between the Jews and Arabs. Instead she puts curbs on fresh Jewish immigration.

1945 After the war thousands of Jewish refugees try to enter Palestine but are refused entry by the British who are worried about the violent Arab opposition to the Jews. Jewish terrorist groups (Irgun and the Stern Gang) try to force Britain to give way.

1947 Britain places the Palestinian problem in the hands of the United Nations. The UN agrees a plan to partition Palestine but both Arabs and Jews reject it.

1948 Britain pulls out of Palestine. The Jews declare that ISRAEL is now an independent state. The Arabs attack them in force but are defeated. During the fighting many Arab civilians are killed and over half a million others flee from the Jewish-held areas of Palestine. These refugees settle in camps, which later become the breeding ground for terrorists and the home of the PLO (Palestine Liberation Organization).

1950 Israel welcomes floods of Jewish immigrants and begins to build a modern state. The Palestinian refugees, who used to live there, are herded into refugee camps near Israel's borders.

1956 President Nasser of Egypt takes over the Suez Canal (upsetting the British and French who own it) and closes it to Israeli shipping. All three countries plan a joint attack and try to seize the Canal, but UN action, and the opposition of the USA and USSR, forces them to withdraw.

1960s Russian influence grows in the Middle East. The Russians help to build Egypt's High Aswan Dam. Russian tanks, planes and weapons help to arm Israel's enemies. The plight of the refugees continues. Terrorist attacks by PLO guerillas harass the Israelis.

1967 Israel, fearing an imminent attack by her Arab neighbours, strikes first and destroys most of the Egyptian Air Force on the ground. Israeli tanks slice through Egypt's Sinai Desert, West Jordan and Syria's Golan Heights. In six days the Arabs are soundly beaten and forced to agree to a truce.

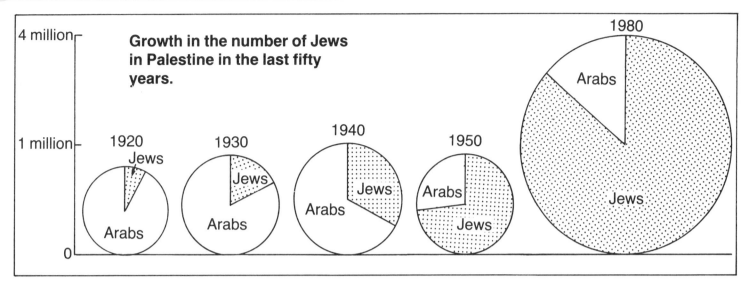

Growth in the number of Jews in Palestine in the last fifty years.

4 million

1 million

0

1920 — Jews / Arabs

1930 — Jews / Arabs

1940 — Jews / Arabs

1950 — Arabs / Jews

1980 — Arabs / Jews

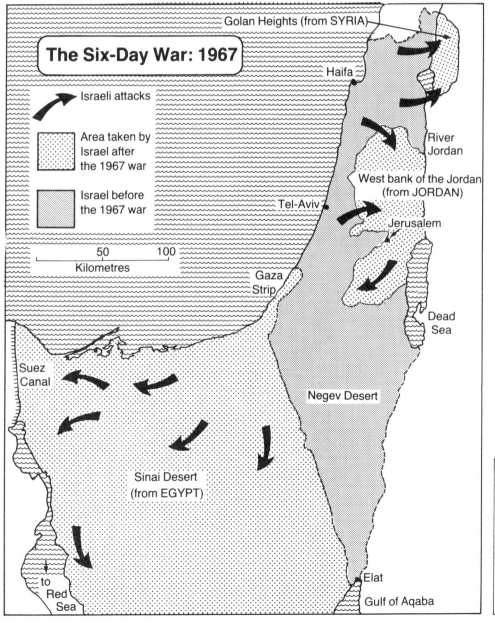

Golan Heights (from SYRIA)

The Six-Day War: 1967

Haifa

→ Israeli attacks

Area taken by Israel after the 1967 war

Israel before the 1967 war

50   100
Kilometres

River Jordan

West bank of the Jordan (from JORDAN)

Tel-Aviv

Jerusalem

Gaza Strip

Dead Sea

Suez Canal

Negev Desert

Sinai Desert (from EGYPT)

Elat

to Red Sea

Gulf of Aqaba

Israel's War of Independence 1948

Lebanon

Syria

Haifa

Iraq

Tel-Aviv

Jerusalem (a divided city)

Jordan

Egypt

Arab attacks 15 May, 1948

Area allocated to Israel by the UN General Assembly 1947

Area taken by Israel after the 1948 war

0   50   100
Kilometres

???????????????????

1 How and why did the Arab-Israeli conflict begin? Why have the Arab countries been so determined to destroy Israel?

2 How have (a) events in Europe, (b) the intervention of the big powers (USA, USSR, UK) affected efforts to solve the Palestine problem?

The Middle East 1967-1982

The Middle East was in turmoil in the 1970s and early 1980s – as you can see from the map opposite. After the Six Day War of 1967 the Russians helped to rearm the Arab armies. Because the Superpowers were supporting opposite sides in the struggle, people feared that more fighting in the Middle East could lead to a Third World War.

Time Line

1972 Arab terrorists seize and murder eleven Israeli athletes at the Munich Olympics.

1973 On Yom Kippur, the holiest day in the Jewish year, the Arabs launch a surprise attack (The Yom Kippur War). Egyptian armies start to advance across the Sinai Desert. The Israeli forces counter-attack and trap the Egyptian Third Army. A truce is then agreed. Peace negotiations follow.

1974 Arab countries use their control of oil production (the Oil Weapon) to get the Western powers to make Israel retreat.

1976 Terrorist attacks on Israel and Israelis. Airliner hijacked to Entebbe airport in Uganda – Israeli commandos rescue hostages. Syrian armies move into the Lebanon to keep peace between Christians and Moslems fighting a bitter civil war.

1979 Camp David peace treaty – Begin (Israel), Sadat (Egypt) and Carter (USA) agree peace treaty between Israel and Egypt. Other Arab countries refuse to take part and condemn Sadat as a traitor. The Israelis agree to leave the Sinai Desert by 1982 and to go back to the pre-1967 boundary between Egypt and Israel.

1979 Islamic Revolution in Iran. Shah is deposed. American Embassy staff in Teheran taken hostage. They are held prisoner for more than a year. American people furious and distressed. In the same year the Russians invade Afghanistan to prevent the collapse of the Communist government there. The Russians fear that the ideas of the Iranian Islamic Revolution could spread to the 25 million Moslems in the Soviet Union. The Islamic Revolution, with its strict Moslem laws, is anti-communist and also anti-Western.

1982 Israel invades Lebanon. More than 10,000 Lebanese civilians are killed, and Lebanese cities are reduced to rubble. The PLO is forced to agree to leave the Lebanon. Israeli troops let Lebanese Christian soldiers into two Palestinian refugee camps (Chatila and Sabra). Hundreds of refugees are slaughtered in cold blood and this leads to worldwide condemnation of Israel for not preventing the massacre.

Results of the Yom Kippur War 1973

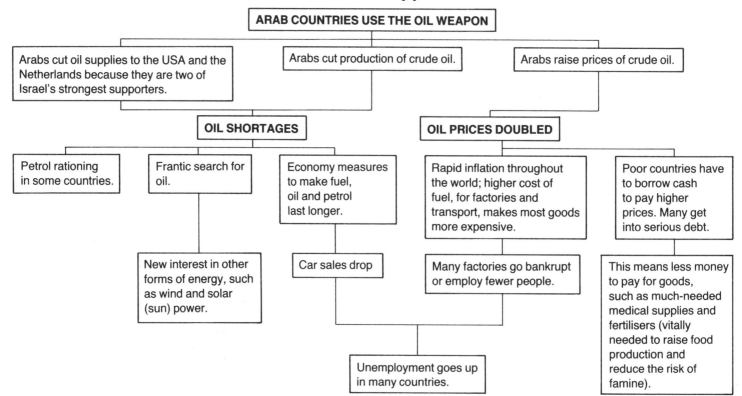

ARAB COUNTRIES USE THE OIL WEAPON

- Arabs cut oil supplies to the USA and the Netherlands because they are two of Israel's strongest supporters.
- Arabs cut production of crude oil.
- Arabs raise prices of crude oil.

OIL SHORTAGES
- Petrol rationing in some countries.
- Frantic search for oil.
- Economy measures to make fuel, oil and petrol last longer.
- New interest in other forms of energy, such as wind and solar (sun) power.
- Car sales drop

OIL PRICES DOUBLED
- Rapid inflation throughout the world; higher cost of fuel, for factories and transport, makes most goods more expensive.
- Poor countries have to borrow cash to pay higher prices. Many get into serious debt.
- Many factories go bankrupt or employ fewer people.
- This means less money to pay for goods, such as much-needed medical supplies and fertilisers (vitally needed to raise food production and reduce the risk of famine).

Unemployment goes up in many countries.

The Middle East in Turmoil 1973-82

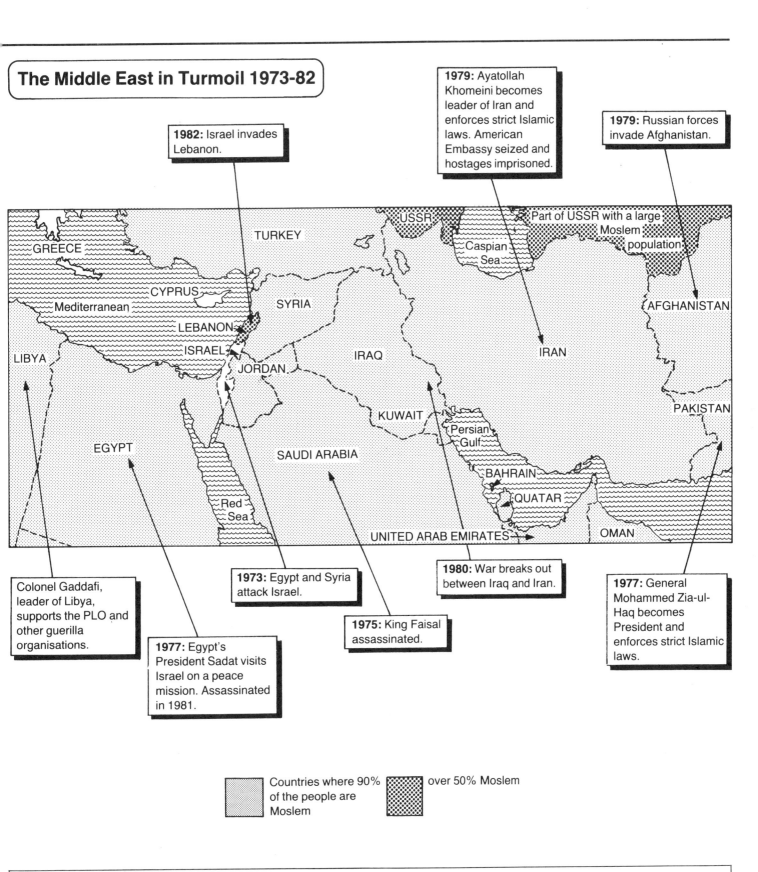

1982: Israel invades Lebanon.

1979: Ayatollah Khomeini becomes leader of Iran and enforces strict Islamic laws. American Embassy seized and hostages imprisoned.

1979: Russian forces invade Afghanistan.

Colonel Gaddafi, leader of Libya, supports the PLO and other guerilla organisations.

1977: Egypt's President Sadat visits Israel on a peace mission. Assassinated in 1981.

1973: Egypt and Syria attack Israel.

1975: King Faisal assassinated.

1980: War breaks out between Iraq and Iran.

1977: General Mohammed Zia-ul-Haq becomes President and enforces strict Islamic laws.

Countries where 90% of the people are Moslem

over 50% Moslem

???

1 What were the consequences of the Yom Kippur War in 1973? Why were the repercussions felt throughout the world?

2 In what ways does the Middle East still pose a threat to world peace?

Problems of our Planet

Urban Problems

All over the world poor peasants, unable to scrape a living from the land, are moving into cities. They are centres of communications, have shops, schools, colleges, hospitals, entertainment, many industries and better chances for good jobs. So most of the world's cities are growing much faster than the population in rural areas. Thirty years ago London and New York were the world's largest cities. Today they have been overtaken by Mexico City, Tokyo, Shanghai, Peking, Moscow, Cairo, Buenos Aires and Seoul (Korea). Many Third World cities have large shanty towns on their outskirts where people have built homes out of rubbish, cardboard boxes, old containers, etc. There are no proper sewers and drains, water supplies or electricity. These appalling city slums can be breeding grounds for disease and violence.

Population

The world's population is growing enormously. In 1930 the world's population was 2,000 million; in 1960 it had reached 3,000 million; and 4,000 million in about 1975. Many countries, such as India and China, have started birth control campaigns to try to reduce the birth rate.

Diseases

Many of the world's peoples live in areas where deadly diseases are common. In some Third World countries a new born baby can only be expected to live to the age of 30-35 years, compared with 75-80 years in highly developed countries like Norway and Sweden. There are not enough modern drugs and medicines; or doctors, nurses, ambulances, hospitals and clinics. But there are now fewer deaths from diseases in the poor countries of the world. WHO (the World Health Organisation) has helped wipe out some diseases (such as smallpox) from the world.

Energy

The world's supplies of oil and gas are rapidly being exhausted. Some experts estimate they will have gone by about the year 2000. Nuclear energy and energy from the sun, tides and winds are not yet able to cope with the problems which will occur when the world's fuel resources are gone.

Education

A large number of the world's peoples are illiterate (unable to read or write). In many Third World countries less than 5% of the population are literate, compared with most of Europe and North America where 99% can read and write. Illiterate people have many problems. For instance they cannot read the instructions for using fertilisers and pesticides, or the safety instructions in a factory.

Conservation and Pollution

The world is being polluted with waste materials such as litter, chemicals in rivers and lakes and smoke fumes in the atmosphere. Many beautiful places have been spoiled by the building of new roads and buildings. We need to look after places and things which are rare, beautiful or unusual. If the Amazon Forest is destroyed it cannot be grown again; if rare animals are hunted and killed, their species may die out and become extinct; if the surviving groups of hunters and farmers in the Amazon Forest are 'civilized' there will be few examples left of the traditional ways of life. When primitive peoples like these are exposed to modern civilisation, they often suffer from 'culture shock' – they cannot adjust to twentieth-century life, such as motorways, cars, aeroplanes, modern working conditions and modern illnesses – and are in danger of dying out altogether.

Water

There is not enough water in some areas, such as those close to the Sahara, Kalahari and Arabian deserts, where many people live. In some years the rainfall is not nearly enough to grow crops. Severe drought causes crop failure, and with it famine, such as those on the fringes of the Sahara desert (the Sahet) in the 1970s. Dams can sometimes be built to conserve water for use in irrigation projects; but they are enormously expensive to build and many Third World countries cannot afford them.

Famine and Farming

Millions of people have died of starvation in the last twenty years. Shortage of food is one of the world's most pressing problems. New farming methods to improve food production are badly needed. In the 1960s and 1970s scientists developed new kinds of wheat and rice which increased grain yields by three or four times. But the new improved crops (the 'Green Revolution') first need fertilisers and pesticides to help them grow. Poor farmers cannot afford these (cost has risen with the price of oil). So the new crops cannot help them.

??????????????????????????????

1 Why have people in many countries become concerned about the problem of environmental pollution and conservation?

2 How, why, and with what reason, has the world attempted to deal with the problem of a rapidly-growing population?

Index